Do you make these mistakes in spelling? Spell a word like

* intercede with an *s*?
* mortgage without the *t*?
* outrageous without the *e*?
* grammar with an *e* instead of an *a* before the final *r*?
* acknowledgment without the *c*? or with an *e* after the *g*? or perhaps with the *d* omitted?
* dilemma with only one *m*? or with an *n*?
* misspelling with only one *s*?

Now you can eliminate such mistakes forever by a proven method which will make you a master speller by teaching you to—SEE THE WORD, THINK THE WORD, FEEL THE WORD, SAY THE WORD, BUILD THE WORD.

"Once again in this book, as he has done in numerous activities as a teacher, Mr. Shefter displays marked ability to pinpoint difficulties and to devise clever, effective methods of meeting them. Readers will profit from the rich talents and broad teaching experience of the author."

*James V. Tague, Principal*
*Port Richmond High School, N.Y.*

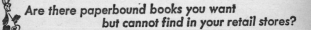

# 6 Minutes a Day to Perfect Spelling

Harry Shefter
*Professor of English*
*New York University*

PUBLISHED BY POCKET BOOKS · NEW YORK

SIX MINUTES A DAY TO PERFECT SPELLING

POCKET BOOK edition published September, 1954
28th printing.........May, 1972

This original POCKET BOOK edition is printed from
brand-new plates made from newly set, clear, easy-to-read type.
POCKET BOOK editions are published by POCKET BOOKS, a division of
Simon & Schuster, Inc., 630 Fifth Avenue, New York, N.Y. 10020.
Trademarks registered in the United States and other countries.
                                                                    L

*To Evelyn*
*and our two little ladies—*
*Barbara and Sharon Ann*

# Table of Contents

*A Word from the Author about*
# You and Spelling

Let me tell you a few things about yourself that you possibly haven't realized before. First of all, there's nothing the matter with you if you have a spelling problem. You are no worse, nor better, than some college instructors, business executives, stenographers, mechanics, and housewives whom I am proud to number among my acquaintances. These people are alert, bright, and conscientious; some of them even have a magnificent command of the English language. But they can't spell!

You aren't therefore a special case. You have lots of company. More than 60% of your classmates, when you went to grade school, worried about their spelling. If you went to college, you will be interested to know that in a recent national survey, conducted among colleges and universities, more than 25% of the students, seniors as well as freshmen, had *serious* spelling troubles with words as easy as "sense." In short, whether you are very young or quite mature, whether you left school early to get a job or went on to get several degrees, neither your educational background nor native intelligence has anything necessarily to do with your ability to spell correctly.

However, you should try to improve your spelling and I'll tell you why in Chapter I.

Here's something else. You are concerned about your spelling, but you never quite get around to doing anything about it except in a haphazard way. Perhaps you've tried to memorize rules, write words out countless times as practice, study long lists of "demons," played "find-the-incorrect-word" games, even fearfully entered spelling bees in the vague hope that somehow you would improve. But you haven't improved because all of these methods are of no value whatever in a long-range plan.

What you need is an organized, fresh attack. That's what you're going to find in this book. The suggested techniques, IF YOU USE THEM, are guaranteed to bring you success—and I do not say this recklessly!

A Greek immigrant, within less than a year after his arrival in this country, was helped to master a list of "Two Hundred Most Frequently Misspelled Words" under the word-a-day plan described in the following pages. When I say "master," I mean he proved he had the words under control for good in frequent writing experiences during the course of his training. What is equally interesting is that while Mr. Costas was concentrating on the selected list he was also picking up numerous other words and adding them to his private collection.

The system has worked with people of all ages. A nine-year-old boy, the son of a colleague of mine, learned how to stop embarrassing his learned father. Twenty-three native-born Americans, ranging in age from 23-57, members of the first class in spelling ever given on the university level, were shown how to get rid of practically all of their troublemakers in less than six months. A television audience of approximately 60,000 people wrote enthusiastic letters about the methods presented before the cameras, and asked that the suggestions be put into book form. As a matter of fact, that's one of the main reasons why *Six Minutes a Day to Perfect Spelling* was written.

I've told you all this because I want to show you that you have it in your power to rid yourself of a frequent source of irritation. However, a word of warning must be inserted here. You will hear it again and again throughout the course of the instructional material. If you merely read each chapter carefully, you will not be any better off at the end than when you started. That is, if you only READ, and do not DO. You will have to cooperate, to do the work as indicated; there's no question about that. But, happily, it's only SIX MINUTES A DAY TO PERFECT SPELLING!

HARRY SHEFTER

# SIX MINUTES A DAY
## TO
# PERFECT SPELLING

# Good Spellers Are Made,
# Not Born!

---

**Please write your name in pencil below:**

---

**Y**ou just wrote your name.

When was the last time you misspelled it? You probably can't remember. Spelling your name is automatic. You do it without thought, without hesitation, knowing it will come out right. *There is no reason, then, why you can't do the same with any word in the English language.*

I'm going to show you how. That's *my* job. I will also tell you how to practice, so that correct spelling can stay with you forever. That will be *your* job. We'll work as a team, and sooner than you dare expect, you will be able to spell any word you want as easily and automatically as you do your name. This is not an idle promise. I have seen it come true time and time again with students in my classrooms.

1

Why does a person always spell his own name correctly? The reason is simply that he has made the words in his name a part of him. He has reduced their spelling to the habit level. Mind you; this is as true of Aleksandra Trzettizorriskaya (a student of mine some years ago) as it is of John Brown, Jack Smith, or you.

It stands to reason then that your spelling will improve when you learn to treat other words the same way. Reduce them to the habit level. Make them a part of you.

Don't worry about long nights of study devoted to impossible-to-remember rules and procedures. This is not that kind of book. All you will need is SIX MINUTES A DAY of your time. All you will have to learn is five simple steps:

## SEE THE WORD!

## THINK THE WORD!

## FEEL THE WORD!

## SAY THE WORD!

## BUILD THE WORD!

That's all: Six minutes a day and five steps.

Let's begin by clearing away some bad spelling alibis. A popular one is that weakness in spelling runs in families. Grandpa had lots of trouble, Papa used to chew the pencil to bits when he wrote, and naturally

Junior can't be expected to do any better. Nonsense! Each slipped into the same bad habit, and not one of them bothered to break it.

Perhaps someone has said to you:

"How can I ever learn to spell? The sounds in the language don't seem to agree with the letters. I write *ENOUGH*. The *GH* sounds like an *F*. Then I find that in *PHONE* the *PH* is also an *F* sound. When I get to *OFTEN*, the *F* is an *F* but the *T* is nothing!"

This kind of poor speller blames our language for his troubles. There are too many silent letters, he says; too many peculiar combinations that don't spell the way they sound.

He seems to have a point. Consider how the English language grew. The ancient history of the British Isles is the record of one invasion after another. About three thousand years ago, the first invaders, variously known as Celts, Gaels, or Britons, made their appearance in Scotland, Ireland, Wales, and England. Although these tribes stayed over nine hundred years, they left little evidence of their language. Less than one percent of the contents of a modern unabridged dictionary can be traced to these earliest inhabitants.

About 55 B.C., Caesar's legions started to bully their way into England. Strangely, however, the strong Latin and Greek influence on English did not occur in the four hundred years of Roman occupation, but came during the revival of learning in the Renaissance period and from eighteenth century classical scholars like Dr. Samuel Johnson.

After the Romans, Teutonic hordes—Angles, Saxons, and Jutes—came storming in. By 500 A.D. the remnants of the original Britons had been driven to obscure regions, and Anglo-Saxon became the foundation of the language we use. Words such as WISDOM, BEGGAR, WEAKLING, and OWNERSHIP, while containing some unclear vowel sounds and doubled consonants, would not have presented very serious problems.

However, in 1066, William the Conqueror's Frenchmen surged across the Channel and began to force new words into the language. BAILIFF, MORTGAGE, EMBELLISH, CHAMOIS, CAMOUFLAGE, and TECHNIQUE are typical words of French ancestry that contain silent letters which baffle poor spellers.

A few centuries later, the delayed Roman influence set in. Examples like AQUARIUM, ASTERISK, ACHIEVEMENT, STATISTICIAN, and CHIROPRACTOR show the kind of "jaw-breakers," as some call them, that began to appear in English. Often mere length of a word or unusual letter combinations are enough to floor the timid. "Looks too tough!" we say.

Even after the thirteen colonies had become the United States, and had adopted the language of their forefathers, borrowing went on freely. We reached into the Scandinavian countries and took RANSACK, DAHLIA, FLOUNDER, and SLEIGH among others. MACARONI, MOTTO, DILETTANTE, and COLONNADE are but a few of the words Italy gave us.

From Spain we appropriated BARBECUE, BRONCHO, LARIAT, SOMBRERO, and others. Hebrew, Arabic, Indian, Persian, Slavic, American Indian, African, and Chinese are additional languages that enriched our vocabulary, but added to our spelling problems.

Is it any wonder that English has no pattern? We take foreign words with complicated letter formations, don't bother to simplify them, and dump them right into the hopper. Then off we go on another merry spelling amboree, or so it seems.

But if this were the basic cause of our troubles, we would just throw up our hands and hope for the best. Actually, scientific studies prove that through the years *most spelling mistakes are made with simple, everyday words.*

The classic collection of frequently misspelled words, found in every grade school speller and called "The Hundred Spelling Demons," is a good example. Take a look at this list at the beginning of the Appendix (pages 181 and 183). Not one of the demons looks frightening, does it? Yet these words, and others like them, give poor spellers most of their headaches.

Poor spelling is, therefore, neither inherited nor completely created by the structure of the language. How DOES it come about? Almost always, the trouble starts early in life AND BECOMES A BAD HABIT.

To be analytical for a moment, here are the stories of real people who let themselves fall into misspelling traps. Each is typical of how a poor speller is made, not born.

### The Case of Mr. A.

He was introduced to the mystery of the written word by a rather grim-faced school teacher. The weekly spelling tests became moments of sheer horror. Poor marks increased his sense of failure. After a while, he unconsciously began to resist the whole annoying business. He fought back by deliberately showing that he didn't care. A certain amount of attention came his way because of his difficulty.

To live up to his reputation young A. developed misspelling into a habit. Today, although he is a reasonably successful salesman, he frequently finds himself embarrassed by his problems with words.

## The Case of Mr. D.

He left school early to open a small store selling automobile accessories. Last year the fourth branch in a modestly-growing chain was introduced. This intelligent, rising business man is an official in the local Kiwanis, has become prominent in church affairs, and two weeks ago was invited to join a committee to draft a new city charter. Since this is the first time his writing and speaking abilities will come under the public eye, he's worried. Up to now, mispronunciations and misspellings have never been too important. Miss Corbett, his secretary, has been discreet about notes that came to her attention from his desk. She quietly revised errors like "probly, fillum, usialy"—all caused by incorrect pronunciations. Now, however, Mr. D. risks open exposure of his slovenly speech and writing. Accurate spelling and proper pronunciation go hand in hand, AND ONE DOES WASH THE OTHER. Our disturbed friend will have to decline the invitation. Until he has improved his verbal skills, he'll have to keep his weaknesses to himself.

## The Case of Miss B.

She is a junior executive in an advertising agency. Everyone predicts a bright future for her. Although her record in college was brilliant, she constantly had trouble with the English courses. The instructors complained that they could not read her work because of her terrible handwriting. And carelessness in this respect led her to sloppy spelling habits. She would become confused when asked whether a particular letter should be "i" or "e," "a" or "o." Now a question that haunts her is: "Will my spelling weakness eventually cost me my job?"

## The Case of Mrs. C.

This lady takes great pride in her sparkling new home in the suburbs. Since she likes to entertain and take part in club activities, she often finds it necessary to send notes and letters. But she dreads the task because it becomes a major undertaking. An hour or so with the dictionary and a floor littered with discarded sheets of stationery have become the symbols of this ordeal. Mrs. C. has just never learned to *see* a word with her *mind* as well as with her eyes. She needs to be trained to visualize so that the letters will not form a filmy blur, and spelling will not become an emotional catastrophe.

## The Case of Mary E.

She is suffering from a serious brain injury. Talking and writing are very trying experiences. She sees words as you would if you held a paper up to a mirror. Often the letters become jumbled. Only her doctor, through his medical skill and knowledge, can be of any real assistance to her.

There they are. Each is an exhibit in a gallery of poor spellers. One has lost his confidence; another can't say the word right, much less spell it; the third let her slipshod penmanship get her into trouble; the fourth hasn't learned to get a mental picture of the word. Yes, there are good reasons why they can't spell and good reasons why they should improve. But only Mary E. needs more than a fresh start. Everyone else can rid himself of his spelling problems by breaking bad habits and substituting good ones.

You've just reviewed the causes of poor spelling. Whatever yours are, get moving in the right direction today. There are lots of things in your favor. For instance, your personal list of "spelling demons" with which you will have to work isn't as long as you think. I dare say that, if you could remember and write down the words you always misspell, you'd come up with fewer than fifty or sixty. Secondly, you really want to do something about your spelling. Otherwise you wouldn't even be reading this. And certainly, if in a short time you can look any word squarely in the eye, it will be worth the effort you make in following the suggestions outlined here.

Let's get down to business. Let's look at the tricks of the trade.

## • II •

## See the Word!

Everybody daydreams. You do, too, we're sure. You sit back now and then and look at that house you will have some day—the one with the green shutters, light brown siding, and brilliant red roses hugging the foundation. Or perhaps you imagine the sensation you will create on a special occasion. You enter a room. All eyes turn toward you. People whisper admiringly. Calmly, almost indifferently, you walk slowly toward a chair, seat yourself, and pretend that you've been accustomed to this sort of attention ever since you were born. You see the details, the colors, everything as if you were actually there.

In effect, what you are doing is looking with your mind rather than with your eyes. And this is the first trade secret of good spellers. They have a mental picture of every word they write. Their hands merely trace the images on paper.

You already have the ability to see with your mind. Now train yourself to apply it to spelling. It's a must! Without developing this technique, progress will be almost impossible. With it, you will remove a major roadblock.

Turn this book over and look at the back cover. Do you see the large 6 in the phrase "6 Minutes A Day" printed in red at the bottom of the cover? Be sure you are seated comfortably and are completely relaxed. Get set to concentrate.

All right. Try to make your mind a blank. Stare very hard at the number and words for ten seconds. Just stare —try not to think—do nothing else.

Now look away toward some dark surface—the wall, floor, that old couch cover. Count five. The image of at least the number should reappear on the blank area. Practice until this happens regularly.

Try this method with other arrangements: a series of colored circles, a strip from the Sunday comics, a design from a gaudy sport shirt. Stare at the pattern for ten seconds, look away, count five, and try to re-create the image on another surface.

After you train yourself to throw a picture with your mind, try it with words. Let's use CALENDAR as the first example.

If you have trouble with the word, you probably misspell it at the DAR syllable. The fact is that people rarely spell a word so badly that it cannot be recognized. Usually, it is one particular part, or only one letter, that causes the spelling problem. Therefore, focus your attention on the part of the word *you* always misspell— the difficult part for you. Your objective is to get rid of the distorted image you have in your mind and to replace it with a clear and correct one.

Write the word in this manner:

calenDAR

Now the difficult part stands out. Look at this image for ten seconds. Remember: just stare. Let the picture sink in.

Again, try to *see* the image on another surface. Count five. Make sure the difficult part shows up most clearly.

On a piece of paper, write out calenDAR rapidly, "looking" at the picture of the word with your mind's eye all the while. Repeat the whole procedure three times.

. . .

Here are some other devices you can use to set up the image:

1. Try colored crayon for the difficult part, and plain ink or pencil for the rest of the letters.

2. Separate the parts, and underline the difficulty:

*cal en dar*

3. Circle the key part:

*calen (dar)*

4. Use the number 2 to remind you that certain words are always written in two parts:

all 2 right

Spellick #1

If you think you've never seen the word "spellick" before, you are right. It was invented for this book. **SIX MINUTES A DAY TO PERFECT SPELLING** is a complete course in itself. The only additional tools you need are a dictionary, a pencil and some paper, things you should already own. There are, however, some other very useful tools which you can build for yourself . . . if you have the time and, more important, if you have the desire to get ahead as fast as possible. We have called these extra devices *spellicks*, the gimmicks or special tricks in this business of learning to spell. *Spellicks* are separated from the rest of the instruction because they are extras rather than musts. But *spellicks* are the *power tools* of spelling. Use them if you possibly can. Here is *spellick* number one:

Cut a piece of *yellow* cardboard about two feet long and about six inches wide. Use this as the background. Cut other pieces of cardboard of the same color into strips about a foot long and three inches wide. On one such strip print, in *black letters*, the word you are studying at the moment. As you print, make the letters of the difficult part twice the size of the others. Now you have an excellent tool for SEEING THE WORD. The black on yellow will greatly sharpen the image. Just lean the background card against a solid object like a book end, and place the word card in front of it.

Of course, you continue the process of staring at the image for ten seconds, looking away, counting five, trying to create a mind picture, and then writing the word out rapidly as you visualize it.

SEE THE WORD with these:

| | | |
|---|---|---|
| arGUMent | ILLiterate | quaRRel |
| barGAIN | judGMent | reCOMMEND |
| sePARate | keroSENE | SECRETary |
| DEStroy | leISure | tempERAture |
| enVELope | manAGE | UNable |
| femiNINE | neCESSary | VINEgar |
| grATEful | oCCasion | wHISTle |
| handKERchief | PARTner | |

**Review Paragraph**

As a review of this chapter, we have prepared a paragraph containing every key word mentioned in the explanatory material. Naturally, the real test of your ability to spell correctly is in your own writing when you are not deliberately being careful. Therefore, we have used the paragraph form, rather than a list, to make the situation as natural as possible.

These essays are not offered as literary gems. The need to keep them short and at the same time have them contain a special group of particular words creates a problem. Nevertheless, the occasional near-nonsense sentence should not interfere with your main objective, which is to use these paragraphs as a test of how much you have learned!

The best method of course is to ask someone to read aloud to you as you write. If you must work on the material by yourself, simply rewrite it. Look at the key words (those words in boldface) *only long enough to identify them,* not long enough to help you spell them. See the difficult part of each word *in your mind,* not in the text as you get to it in the sentence. Use the blank spaces below the paragraph to jot down the words you missed. Study these again!

If you wish to study a typical **feminine argument,** I recommend that you visit a **bargain** counter. You will see how two shoppers can sometimes **manage** to get into a **quarrel** over even a **handkerchief.** In the **judgment** of each unwilling **partner,** she simply must have the article for her **leisure** moments. On one **occasion** I saw the **temperature** of a **secretary** go up as if it were lighted **kerosene.** She had picked up a **calendar** in an **envelope,** but a bystander had been **unable** to resist reaching for it, too. One would have thought both were illiterate from the looks washed in vinegar that passed between them. Each surely would have been grateful if she had been able to destroy the other. It looked for a moment as if a whistle would have to be blown to separate the pair, but a saleslady made everything all right when she pointed out that the item was not even for sale.

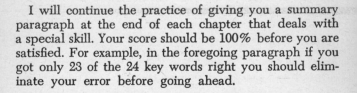

I will continue the practice of giving you a summary paragraph at the end of each chapter that deals with a special skill. Your score should be 100% before you are satisfied. For example, in the foregoing paragraph if you got only 23 of the 24 key words right you should eliminate your error before going ahead.

A word or two about tests in general, and spelling tests in particular. In most areas of information, it is customary to use an examination to measure general knowledge in the field. In school subjects, for example, the traditional 65% or higher indicates satisfactory achievement. Similarly, a mark of 85% might be excellent on a state professional or civil service examination.

But such grades in a spelling test would be meaningless! They would indicate only the percentage of words that need further study. The speller cannot be satisfied with 85% or 90% or 98%. He must strive for 100% EVERY TIME.

You will not, therefore, find any tests here designed merely to allow you to get a score. All the sentences and paragraphs at the ends of chapters or in the appendix are there to help you learn two things:

> the words you still have to study,

> the words you have already mastered.

Toying with long lists of deliberately-misspelled examples of errors or picking out the correct forms from several possibilities is an utter waste of time. In fact, it is dangerous to concentrate your attention on the *wrong* spelling at any time. Your mind may not choose to remember the right one the next time you have to use the word! For this reason, there are no distorted spellings or useless tests in this book.

SEE THE WORD,

*now* . . .

# Think the Word!

Look very quickly at each of the ten words listed below. In the space provided write the first thing that pops into your mind. Try to make your response as automatic as you can.

| | | | |
|---|---|---|---|
| AUNT | _____ | FEAR | _____ |
| BLUE | _____ | GIRL | _____ |
| CARE | _____ | HEAD | _____ |
| DUTY | _____ | IRON | _____ |
| EASE | _____ | JUNE | _____ |

Now examine each combination, the original word and the one you inserted. What made AUNT suggest

_____ to you? Think about it for a moment. If you wrote the name of a person in the space, isn't she the one you like best, or possibly never could tolerate? If you wrote SAD after BLUE, isn't it that the color depresses you for one reason or another? If you put CHAIR or COUCH after EASE, you probably identify relaxation with a favorite piece of furniture. But no matter what you wrote down, by filling in the spaces, you participated in what psychologists call an "association of ideas."

This term applies to a very basic human characteristic. The faculty of your mind that helps you remember things is constantly establishing these BONDS. It explains why the strains of a familiar bit of music can bring back a picture of a wonderful evening you once spent; why you'll reject a certain kind of food because it makes you think, perhaps subconsciously, of those harrowing mornings you spent on the high chair struggling with your persistent mother; why the number 16 may mean a dreamy birthday party to a girl.

In the ability of your mind to associate lies the key to another secret of good spelling. You have learned how to get a mental picture of the difficult part of a word. Now if you can place a mental string around your finger in addition to the image in your mind, the result will be startling. When you tie in the problem syllable with an instantly-recalled idea, you will have another strong aid toward the proper spelling of a word. The secret is simply to form a BOND.

Let's go back to CALENDAR, the example we used to point out how advisable it is to *see* the word with the *mind* as well as the *eye*. The A between the D and R is the trouble-maker. Now invent a statement that creates a BOND between the difficult part and an easily-remembered idea. For example: According to the calenDAR, the D. A. R. will meet this week. There it is. The abbreviation of the name of the famous feminine group reminds you of the A between the D and R. It can even be an entertaining game. The rules are simple:

1. Set up the association.

2. Make it as silly or unusual as you can. Oddly enough, one tends to remember nonsense more readily than logic.

3. Try to combine this association with an image in your mind as explained in the previous chapter. See the word AND think the word! Thus you make the difficult part of the word both the basis for the IMAGE and the association for the **BOND.**

4. Once you've decided on a good combination, study it for ten seconds, look away toward another surface, SEE AND THINK the problem syllable, and then write the whole word out rapidly.

Take a look at these additional examples. After you have become thoroughly familiar with the method, gradually make up a list of your own.

1. It is VILE to allow special priVILEge.
2. The suit on the SERGEANT looked like SERGE on an ANT.
3. She screamed, "EEE!" as she passed the cEmEtEry.
4. The VILLAIN enjoyed his VILLA IN the hills.
5. Scientists LABOR in a LABORatory.
6. GM (General Motors) sent an acknowledGMent.
7. Every AGE has its trAGEdy.
8. You GAIN when you buy a barGAIN.
9. My PROF is called PROFessor Gordon.
10. He lost his TEMPER AT the rise in TEMPERATure.
11. Don't MAR your writing with bad gramMAR.
12. Draw ALL the lines parALLel.
13. There was constant rePETition of his PET phrase.
14. TEN times later his persisTENce was rewarded.

15. She flew into a RAGE at his outRAGEous remarks.

16. EMMA was in a dilEMMA.

17. When I think of FeBRuary, I say, "BR!"

18. It was an ERA of great litERAture.

19. The princiPAL is my PAL.

20. You RILE me with your sacRILEgious remarks.

21. StationERy is for a lettER.

22. When he ATE, he was grATEful.

23. "ACH!" There goes the parACHute.

24. My skin shows resisTANce to TAN.

25. He would sooner DIE than be obeDIEnt.

It may occur to you at this point that some of the BONDS don't seem to help you very much. This is as it should be. The bonds must be made up BY YOU! You will remember what YOU have created far better than something thought of by another person.

Here again is the summary paragraph. Try it after you have mastered the foregoing group of words. Remember: it is better if this material is dictated to you.

## Review Paragraph

Early in February an **acknowledgment** written on official **stationery** came from the **laboratory.** By this time the police chief's **temperature** was at the boiling point. The **tragedy** of the torn **parachute,** discovered by the **persistence** of Sergeant Bristol, remained unsolved. The **villain** was still at large, and there wasn't even a **principal** suspect. But the chief had faced a **dilemma** before. In **grammar** which a **professor** would never use and a minister might call **sacrilegious** he ordered his men to search every part of the city, even the **cemetery**, and to break down the **resistance** of anyone brought in. The **outrageous** crime had no **parallel** in the **literature** of murder, but it is the **privilege** of a seldom **grateful** public to demand results. Police chiefs are **obedient** to a public mood, and in this case the public, fearing a **repetition** of the crime, was in no mood to **bargain.**

_____

_____

_____

_____

_____

_____

Spellick #2

If you have no one available to dictate these paragraphs, there is still a way to solve the problem. Try to borrow a recording machine. Perhaps a friend has one. Then you can simply record the material in this and other chapters. Thereafter, you can play back the paragraphs at your leisure, and write as you listen. You will find the page numbers of all the summary paragraphs in the index for quick reference.

There are many advantages to such an arrangement. The fact that you hear YOUR OWN VOICE dictating should help you remember. You can play the tape or record as often as you like, stop whenever you please, and even make up essays of your own for further tests. If you use this suggestion, be careful to observe these cautions for the actual recording:

1. Speak clearly into the microphone; pronounce extra-carefully. Do not leave out any syllables or letters.

2. Break up the sentences into phrases. For example:

   "Early in February — an acknowledgment — written on official stationery — came from the laboratory —"

3. Read slowly; pause long enough after each phrase to allow yourself time to write it. You can accustom yourself to the proper timing by practicing writing sentences as you read them aloud. When you think you have the tempo set, and you begin to record, ALLOW A FEW MORE SECONDS AT EACH BREAK.

4. Identify each paragraph at the beginning of the recording. Say something like: "This is the paragraph on page —." You may want to check a word or sentence at a future date, and fail to remember the source. It would be wise to repeat this information on the label, if you've used a disc, or on the outside of the container, if you did the job on tape.

5. If you aren't satisfied with a particular recording, DO IT OVER. Unless you feel comfortable as you listen, the recorded material will be more of a hindrance than a help!

So far you have learned to SEE THE WORD in your mind and THINK THE WORD by association. Now let's turn to the third important method of solving your spelling problems.

## · IV ·

## Feel the Word!

Have you ever watched a blind person become familiar with a strange object? He goes over the outline of the figure carefully and slowly. *Through his fingers* he is memorizing the shape. When he feels something similar again, his sense of touch will immediately identify it. In fact, this is the way a blind person learns to read Braille. But all of us have the ability to "think" and "see" with our fingers. Here are two illustrations.

You sit in a darkened movie theater. As you watch the film, you hear clicking sounds nearby. You are puzzled, but when the lights go on you discover a woman putting her knitting away. Her *fingers* have been busy in the dark while her mind was concentrating on the screen.

One morning you are late. As you dash down the steps, your fingers feverishly make a knot in your tie. Your mind, already forming excuses for tardiness, doesn't spend a second's thought on your tie. Your *fingers* are doing the thinking.

Or let me remind you about the signature you wrote on the first page. You didn't think about it. You let your *fingers* take charge. Your mind was probably wondering why you were asked to do the job.

There are many things you do almost entirely by reflex. The patterns of behavior are so habitual that your mind often operates in a secondary capacity. It has such a clear picture of the necessary movements and such a strong association with the proper reactions that the physical process becomes prompt, efficient, and almost unthinking.

You know how to SEE THE WORD. You know how to THINK THE WORD. Learn how to FEEL THE WORD and spelling will also become one of your mechanically perfect skills.

This physical attack upon words is designed to force the hand to do most of the work of spelling. It is almost the final step in enabling you to write any word as casually as you do your signature.

Try another experiment. Write the number *19836* on a blank piece of paper. Put your finger on each digit and trace it, saying it aloud as you trace. Do this three times. Turn the paper over and write the original number once more, but, as you do, say aloud *12345*. If you can write one number while saying another, you have proved that your hand can be taught to spell automatically.

This skill is particularly useful for words that contain more than one difficult part. A *bond* or *image* may not be enough to eliminate all the trouble spots.

Take the word PSYCHOLOGY, for example. A poor speller may forget that it begins with a P, or that it contains a Y and CH. It is therefore possible to make several errors. The attack must be on an over-all basis. You must *feel* the *entire* word and be able to write it mechanically.

Use this system:

1. On a piece of paper, write the word in large, well-rounded, *script* letters. About twice the size of your normal handwriting should be sufficient.

*psychology*

2. Place the pen or pencil you have used aside, and, WITH YOUR FINGER directly touching the letters, slowly TRACE the word, softly repeating aloud each letter as you trace it.

3. Allow no break in the rhythm. Your arm should swing along, not stopping its motion until it has completed the word. Dot the *i* or cross the *t*, if there is one.

4. Do this three times. Start carefully, and gradually increase the pace until it is very much like the speed at which you normally write.

5. After you have been able to sweep through the word confidently, without pausing, turn the paper over. THIS IS VERY IMPORTANT. SAY ANYTHING ALOUD AS YOU WRITE OUT THE WORD. Repeat your name and address, or recite a favorite bit of poetry, or simply count. You want to grasp the word in a physical sense. The hand, not the mind, must do the spelling. By talking as you write, you force yourself to make the process automatic.

6. If you make the slightest mistake, repeat the exercise until your HAND spells the word. Remember: use your finger to trace. Do not use a pen or pencil.

Here are a few more words that contain problems in several places. They can be handled best by the tracing method.

1. *minimum*
2. *campaign*
3. *ridiculous*
4. *guardian*
5. *bureau*
6. *ascertain*
7. *memorandum*
8. *mortgage*
9. *guarantee*
10. *acknowledge*

After a while, you will find that you can combine tracing with the two other techniques of seeing and thinking. Thus, if you must think about the spelling, it will help rather than hinder the writing.

Here is the easy way to combine the three steps:

1. Construct the image in your mind as suggested in the second chapter.
2. Prepare a BOND for the difficult part or parts of the word.
3. Trace the word WITH YOUR FINGER three times.
4. Write it rapidly AS YOU LOOK AT THE IMAGE IN YOUR MIND and REPEAT THE BOND ALOUD. In this way, you will be **seeing the word, thinking the word,** and **feeling the word** all at once.

If you can master this three step technique, 90% of your spelling troubles will be over.

## Review Paragraph

And now the summary paragraph:

Lucy looked at Mr. Forbes, her **guardian.** She felt that the terms of the **mortgage** were **ridiculous,** and she clearly recalled the **memorandum** the head of the housing **bureau** had sent her. He had strongly urged some sort of **guarantee** of payments so that the risks would be at a **minimum.** She realized she would first have to **ascertain** what **psychology** would work best before she could start a **campaign** to force Mr. Forbes to **acknowledge** the justice of her claim.

_____

_____

_____

SEE THE WORD!

THINK THE WORD!

FEEL THE WORD!

*and . . .*

## · V ·

## Say the Word!

**H**ere's an old time vaudeville joke, but there's more than a laugh buried in it.

A man goes into a restaurant and sits down at a table.
"I'll have some **kidley** stew," he says.
"Pardon, sir," suggests the waiter, "but don't you mean **kidney** stew?"
"I said **kidley** stew, did'l I?" replies the man.

It is very common for people to be entirely unaware of the spoken mistakes they make. These people haven't learned to listen to themselves talk. Unfortunately, oral errors are often transferred to written words. Many misspellings come directly from faulty pronunciation.

You tend to write the way you speak. Examine these:

SURPRISE             FILM

CAVALRY              JEWELRY

Say each one aloud. Try to listen to yourself as you speak. If you have trouble concentrating on your voice, use this simple device. Stand a few inches away from a wall. Hold your hands behind your ears and parallel to the wall. As you talk, you will hear the sounds as if they were coming over a microphone.

Now that you have pronounced the words, look them up in a good dictionary. You will notice that, after the spelling of a word, its proper pronunciation is indicated by certain symbols for the vowels and consonants. At the bottom of each page of text of the better dictionaries is listed the key or interpretation of these signs. Become familiar with them, but there is no need to learn the list by heart. Frequent use will fix the various marks in your memory. Also glance through the "Guide to Pronunciation" and "The Rules for Syllabication" usually found in the introductory matter. Learn how to use this information when necessary.

All right, you've checked the words. Did you leave out a syllable? Did you add one? Did you fail to say R in SURPRISE? Did you put the L before the V in CAVALRY? If you made any of these mistakes, you committed one of a number of common spoken errors that often become spelling errors.

The problem breaks down into four types of mispronunciation.

## A. Extra Syllable

Some letter combinations in our language are difficult to produce orally. An M following an L is an example. The open mouth position must immediately be followed by closed lips, and stopped short. The tendency, therefore, is to add a syllable between the two letters to try to bridge the gap. Thus we get FILLUM instead of FILM.

You can train yourself to speak correctly. Slow down your speech. Give each sound its full value before producing another. If you are in doubt about a word, or you hear other people saying it differently, look it up. Practice before a mirror. Watch your lip and jaw movements. Say it right and you will spell it right!

SAY AND SPELL:

| | | |
|---|---|---|
| ATHLete | disasTRous | rememBRance |
| launDRy | hinDRance | barbaROUS |
| umBRella | mischieVOUS | |

attacKED
*E is not pronounced*

drowNED
*E is not pronounced*

## B. Omitted Syllable

It is just as wrong, of course, to leave out a syllable. Here the trouble arises out of speech that is too hurried. Slow up. Take it easy. Say the whole word. Don't say and write JOOLERY instead of JEWELRY.

SAY AND SPELL:

| | | |
|---|---|---|
| accidentALly | poEM | tempERature |
| probABly | choCOlate | labORatory |

## C. Incorrect and Omitted Sounds

You may occasionally use the proper number of syllables in a word, but pronounce a particular letter incorrectly or leave it out altogether. You must not be careless. Get the dictionary habit. Don't say and spell SUPPRISE when you mean SURprise.

SAY AND SPELL:

| | | |
|---|---|---|
| arCtic | diPHtheria | goverNment |
| FebRuary | sacrilEgious | quesTION |

## D. Reversed Sounds

Usually this error occurs as the result of hearing the word spoken incorrectly and copying the mispronunciation without bothering to check. In this way the little boy listens to his friend describe the charge of the "calvary," and may imitate this form for years before discovering that the word is CAVALRY. And imagine his dismay when he learns that there really is a word CALVARY, the hill where Christ was crucified!

SAY AND SPELL:

| | |
|---|---|
| irrELEvant | trAGEdy |
| PERform | PERspiration |

Right here there must be a question in your mind.

"What if I can say the word correctly, but still have trouble spelling it?"

That's fair enough. But don't forget the first three techniques. When you have removed the speech problem, treat the word like any other. SEE IT, THINK IT, FEEL IT! It's the basic attack. What we're doing now is giving you hints that can be applied to groups of words. However, the SEE-THINK-FEEL method is the guaranteed way, even if no other suggestion helps.

•        •        •

Now come additional problems related to speech.

## E. The Indefinite Vowel

You know what a vowel is—a, e, i, o, u, or y (as in many and mystery). Because of the different sounds each of these can be—for example, A as in bay, bat, ball, b*a*r, b*a*re—the pronunciation does not always tell us what the proper letter is. This is especially true in words where the middle vowel sound is little more than a grunt. In RELATIVE, merely pronouncing the word does not clearly tell us that an A should follow the L.

Suppose, however, whenever you have to spell RELATIVE you also think of RELATE (here the A is sharply marked). Then RELATIVE becomes easy. You can use this technique with many words that fall into this class —words where the middle vowel sound is not clear, but where it *is* clear in a word from the same family.

Note these:

|  | Word | First Cousin |
|---|---|---|
| A | narrative | narrate |
|  | sedative | sedate |
|  | miracle | miraculous |
| E | arithmetic | arithmetical |
|  | competition | compete |
|  | celebration | celebrity |
| I | definite | define |
|  | compilation | compile |
|  | hypocrisy | hypocritical |
| O | frivolous | frivolity |
|  | revolution | revolt |
|  | consolation | console |
| U | exultation | exult |
|  | sulphur | sulphuric |
|  | future | futurity |

·          ·          ·

You have probably had your troubles with the next group of speech–spelling puzzlers. These are words that come in pairs, or even appear as threesomes; they are pronounced exactly alike, or very nearly so, but have essential differences in meaning and spelling. You want to talk about a *stationary* object. You know that there is one word that uses an A and another that uses an E in the final syllables.

To handle these we go back to the THINK THE WORD method. Create a bond between the difficult part and some bit of nonsense. Treat each word as if it were a separate unit and you will avoid confusion.

### F. Think the Words That Sound Alike!

Look at these:

1. StationAry objects stAnd still.
   StationEry is used for lEttErs.

2. A princiPAL should be a PAL.
   The principAl idea is the mAin one.
   GrapPLE a princiPLE to your heart.

3. I can't EAT in hot wEATher.
   I don't know WHETher pie will WHET my appetite.

4. A grOAN is a loud mOAN.
   When I am grOWN I shall OWN a store.

5. I hEAR with my EAR.
   We looked hERE, thERE, everywhERE.

Some words are not even pronounced alike but are close enough to be troublesome.

Watch out for:

    accept-except                 prophecy-prophesy

| affect-effect | moral-morale |
| angel-angle | canvas-canvass |
| council-counsel | loose-lose |
| quiet-quite | desert-dessert |

Sometimes, in an effort to be informal or conversational, a speaker or writer will use contractions. These are single words that have been made out of two. For example, IT IS becomes IT'S in the contracted form. We have, in effect, substituted an apostrophe (') for the letter I between the T and the S and made one word. Do not confuse this with ITS, the form that does not use the *apostrophe* and which indicates possession. Whenever you are in doubt about ITS or IT'S, try the sentence using the two words IT IS. If they fit, IT'S is correct; if they do not, use ITS.

Put this book in it's or its place.

Substitute IT IS. Does it make sense? It doesn't, of course. Use its in its place.

Note: There is no such form as ITS'.

This test also applies to your and you're, who's and whose, and their, there and they're.

Here are some examples:

Your or you're not wanted here.
(Try you are. It fits. Therefore, use you're.)

Your or you're name is John.
(Try you are. It doesn't fit. Use your.)

I wonder who's or whose the winner.
(Try who is. It fits. Therefore, use who's.)

I know who's or whose hat that is.
(Try who is. It doesn't fit. Use whose.)

Their or there or they're coming Sunday.
(Try they are. It fits. Therefore, use they're.)

Their or there or they're is the place we stayed last year.
(Try they are. It doesn't fit. Use there. Indicates place.)

Their or there or they're team won.
(Try they are. It doesn't fit. Use their. Indicates possession.)

Remember:

It's SHOULD'VE or SHOULD HAVE
    but never should of!

•            •            •

You've tried spelling rules before. You probably gave up in disgust, too. There were so many exceptions that you finished by being more harmed than helped. That's why we're going to bother with only those rules that work so often and with so many words that exceptions are of no consequence.

This brings us to the most valuable spelling rule in the language. It, too, is tied in with pronunciation. We'll review certain speech principles first, and afterwards show how they apply in spelling to a vast number of words.

## G. Accented Syllable Rule—(when to double final consonants)

Vowels—We've talked about these before: A, E, I, O, U, and sometimes Y.

Consonants—All the other letters in the alphabet. Observe
that the U in EQUIP has the effect of a W. When U
is pronounced W it is properly considered a consonant.

Accent—A syllable is that part of a word that is said all at
once, without a break or pause in the rhythm. It
might be compared to a musical note. We say the
word STOP in one continuous sound, and it would be
represented in music by one note. Its technical name
is MONOSYLLABLE (MONO—from the Greek meaning one). POLYSYLLABLES (POLY—many) are words
that contain two or more syllables or pauses. In
music, we would need two notes to represent REMIT
(two syllables RE-MIT) and three for PREFERENCE
(three syllables PRE-FER-ENCE). When we pronounce a single-syllable word (monosyllable), we
place the same amount of stress on the whole word.
However, in polysyllables, only one of the syllables
receives the stress. When we pronounce polysyllabic
words, we use added volume or loudness on the
syllable custom has dictated should receive what we
call the accent.

reMIT—Added volume or loudness is placed on the
second syllable.

LAbel—The first syllable receives the greater stress
or accent.

PREFerence—Here again the first syllable is accented.
Note, however, how there is an accent shift to
the second syllable in preFER, even though
preference and prefer are in the same word
family.

Spellick #3

If you aren't sure whether you are stressing the proper syllable, even when you know from a dictionary which it should be, here is a good test. Get any flat piece of glass—a small mirror, a medicine chest shelf, or a plate. Sprinkle a little powder along the surface. Now hold the powdered piece of glass about a half inch from your lips. As you speak you'll notice that a puff of powder will be blown forward when you accent a particular syllable. Let the puff tell you whether the stress came at the right time. At first, deliberately overdo the accenting, expelling the breath with violence so that you will have no difficulty recognizing the point at which you increased the volume.

·　　　·　　　·

We are now ready for the accented syllable rule, the most valuable of all spelling rules.

Observe these two groups of words:

| | |
|---|---|
| DIF fer | oc CUR |
| LA bel | ad MIT |
| ED it | ex PEL |

**Similarities:**

1. Each word ends in a single consonant.
2. Each final single consonant is preceded by a single vowel.

**Major Differences:**

1. In the group on the right, the accent falls on the last syllable.

2. In the group on the left, the accent falls on the first syllable.

**Rule:**

IF A WORD ENDS IN ONE CONSONANT PRECEDED BY A SINGLE VOWEL,

IF THE SYLLABLE IN WHICH THIS COMBINATION APPEARS IS ACCENTED,

DOUBLE THE FINAL CONSONANT BEFORE ADDING A SYLLABLE BEGINNING WITH A VOWEL.

·     ·     ·

IF THE SYLLABLE IN WHICH THE COMBINATION APPEARS IS *NOT* ACCENTED, DO *NOT* DOUBLE.

We can condense the rule into a formula:

FSA *equals* DOUBLE!

F—final single consonant
S—single vowel preceding
A—accent on the combination

Let's put the FSA rule into practice. From the groups used as examples above, take the word OCCUR. It ends in an R (single final consonant), the R is preceded by U (single vowel), and the stress falls on CUR (accent on the combination).

**Therefore:**

ocCUR *plus* ED (syllable beginning with a vowel) *equals* occuRRed (doubled final consonant)

*OR*
ocCUR *plus* ENCE *equals* occuRRence

*OR*

occCUR *plus* ING *equals* occuRRing

**However**

Take the word DIFFER from the column on the left. There is the final consonant R, and there is the single vowel E, but the stress falls on DIF—which is NOT THE SYLLABLE CONTAINING THE COMBINATION!

**Therefore:**

DIFfer *plus* ED *equals* diffeRed.
DIFfer *plus* ENCE *equals* diffeRence.
DIFfer *plus* ING *equals* diffeRing.

The consonant is not doubled because the accent does not fall on the syllable containing the single final consonant preceded by a single vowel.

Here's what happens to the rest of the columns.

| Last Syllable Not Accented | Last Syllable Accented |
| --- | --- |
| LAbel, labeLed, labeLing | adMIT, admiTTed, admiTTance |
| EDit, ediTed, ediTing | exPEL, expeLLed, expeLLing |

In single syllable words you don't have to worry about the accent since the stress automatically falls on the entire word. All you do is decide whether there is a single final consonant preceded by a single vowel.

stop, stoPPing, stoPPed
bat, baTTing, baTTed
flat, flaTTer, flaTTen

**But**

meet, meeTing (two vowels precede the final consonant)

We talked about accent shifts a little while ago. Notice what happens to the word PREFER when the stress changes from one syllable to another.

preFER, prefeRRed, prefeRRing

**And**

PREFeRence (accent shifted to first syllable, no doubling)

Exceptions? Yes, there are some:

### Double L's Instead of Single

canceLLation                    crystaLLize
chanceLLor                      exceLLent

### French Endings

crocheTed                       ricocheTed

(Note: Both words end in the AY sound, so that it is actually a vowel ending.)

### Double Words

overlaPPed                      outfiTTed

(Note: The first consists of OVER and Lap, has almost a double accent; therefore, this and others like it are treated as if the second half determines the spelling.)

### Unreasonable Ones

chagriNed                       gaSeous

(That's right; there seems to be no reason why the single letters are used, but there they are!)

●          ●          ●

### Suggestion:

If you want to remember the exceptions, set up BONDS for them; then SEE and FEEL them:

1. The chanCELLor gave an exCELLent reason for his canCELLation of the talk on the plant CELL.

2. CrocheTed and ricocheTed suit me to a T.

3. He overlaPPed his authority and overstePPed his bounds.

4. I had to GRIN when he was chaGRINed.

5. GASeous is the adjective of GAS.

**Suggestion:**

Ordinarily, rules with many exceptions are worthless. That's why such rules have been left out of this book. Certainly, it's easier to use the SEE-THINK-FEEL method. However, the ACCENTED SYLLABLE rule works with so many hundreds of words that it's one you ought to make a real effort to learn. Give it a try.

FSA *equals* DOUBLE CONSONANT (before added syllable beginning with a vowel).

Now practice with these:

| Word | Add: ED | Word | Add: ING |
|------|---------|------|----------|
| comMIT | _____ | beGIN | _____ |
| conTROL | _____ | reFER | _____ |
| Open | _____ | LEVel | _____ |
| CAter | _____ | OFfer | _____ |

| Word | Add: ER | Word | Add: ANCE |
|------|---------|------|-----------|
| REVel | _____ | adMIT | _____ |
| FAT | _____ | reMIT | _____ |

| Word | Add: OR | Word | Add: ENCE |
|------|---------|------|-----------|
| BET | _____ | conFER | _____ |
| | | | (Watch shift!) |
| EDit | _____ | inFER | _____ |

**Answers:** committed, controlled, opened, catered, beginning, referring, leveling, offering, reveler, fatter, admittance, remittance, bettor, editor, conference, inference.

Now the review paragraphs. Don't try them until you have studied the material in this chapter carefully. One look is not enough. Only when you are sure of each section are you ready to test yourself. Remember: any mistakes, back you go to the explanation. The letter before each paragraph refers to the section where the words originally appeared in this chapter.

## Review Paragraphs

**A.** Before going for his **laundry**, the **athlete** decided to attend the recent **film** which told the story of how **barbarous** tribes had once **attacked** the ancient Romans in the **disastrous** period of their decline. As he watched the picture, a **mischievous** little girl kept poking him with an **umbrella**. This proved quite a **hindrance** to his efforts to follow the scenes of **drowned** soldiers and burning houses. In his **remembrance**, he could not recall when he had been more annoyed.

_____

_____

_____

**B.** Dr. Jones **accidentally** dropped the box of **chocolates** on his way home from the **laboratory**. However, he still had the **jewelry** for his wife, along with the birthday **poem,** so he knew her **temperature** wouldn't rise.

**C.** Because of the **arctic** blasts common in **February**, it is no **surprise** that people recovering from **diphtheria** are told by doctors to stay indoors. In answer to a **question,** a **government** health agency agreed that this was wise. It would be almost **sacrilegious** to ignore both official and medical advice.

**D.** It is not **irrelevant** at this time to say that the **cavalry** has limited use today. The men who ride to war on horseback, however, do **perform** important jobs in hilly areas. Sending a tank up a steep pass would be inviting **tragedy**. With a little **perspiration** mounted troops overcome such obstacles.

_____

_____

_____

_____

_____

_____

**E.** School had begun to act like a **sedative** on Bob. Preparing **sulphur** in his chemistry class, struggling with **arithmetic** problems, or reading how the **hypocrisy** of certain kings had led to **revolution** no longer interested him. He prayed for an academic **miracle** which would make the **compilation** of facts a **frivolous** task and destroy the **competition** for marks which brought **exultation** only to the brighter students. There was **consolation** in the future, however. A **relative** had sent Bob an **invitation** to spend the summer on a ranch. He eagerly glanced over his uncle's **narrative** of what they would do out west. Now he could look forward to a **definite celebration** from school work.

**F.** The **weather** was almost perfect. **Here** and **there** slivers of sunlight shot through the **stationary** branches like silver darts. **Everywhere** I could **hear** birds calling to one another. **There** was also the croaking of frogs to add a bass section to the **principal** theme of the forest concert. I wondered **whether** I should waste my time scrawling words on the **stationery** that lay in my lap. Then I thought of George's last letter:

"**It's** clear that **you're** like most people without **principle** whose main job seems to be to excuse **their** failure to write. **They're** expert at telling what they **should've** done, but **who's** to say why they didn't. This is **your** last chance. No reply this time and you'd better forget my address and **its** owner!"

I put pen to paper. Nature would have to wait.

_____

_____

_____

**G.** The **editor** opened the **conference** by **leveling** a charge. Someone had **committed** the crime of **offering** a **bettor** a chance to make his profits **fatter** by showing him **preference** to **controlled** information. In fact, the **meeting** had been called by Mr. Grimes to mark the **beginning** of his campaign for **stopping** the release of news as it **occurred** and before it was **edited.**

"You can draw your own **inference**," he said. "I haven't **labeled** anyone, but it makes no **difference** to me who has **catered** to dishonest men. Whether he has received a **remittance** for his help or not, he will be **expelled**, and will never gain **admittance** to this office again. I'm **referring** to all when I say I would just as soon hire a drunken **reveler** as allow one of you to **flatten** the reputation of this paper. You've **batted** out of turn if you think I'm fooling."

---

---

Do not go on to the next chapter until you can spell each of the 89 key words correctly.

SEE THE WORD!

THINK THE WORD!

FEEL THE WORD!

SAY THE WORD!

*and finally . . .*

# Build the Word!

A word is like a rubber band. It can be stretched, pushed together, or left in its original shape. Its job in a sentence determines what form it will take.

Love is not alone for the **lovely**. **Loveliness** of heart can **lovelier** be by far than of face, ofttimes **loved** briefly, but soon **loveless** and **lovelorn**—the **loveknot** broken, the **lovebird** flown, and the **lovers** parted. Then no **loving** hands will help the **lovesick** curl **lovable** hair into **lovelock** long.

This amorous adventure into word study brings us to the relationship between grammar and spelling. Writing a word correctly is sometimes only the beginning. It proves you know one form. However, you must learn all the other forms before you really have the situation and your spelling well in hand. You must become acquainted with a word's whole family tree, technically called the parts of speech. Let's see what the names of some of them are.

## A. The Noun

This is the main thing we talk about in a sentence:

The **chair** is quite new.

or is part of a short group of words, called a phrase:

We walked (into the **woods**).

or may come at the end to help finish the thought:

I lifted the **box**.

or may appear in all three places at once:

The **launching** of the **ship** pleased the **town**.

Fundamentally, it is a name of:

1. A Person—John is my brother.
2. A Place—My home is in New York.
3. A Thing—A shoe is packed in a box.
4. An Idea—Peace feeds on justice and understanding.
5. An Activity—Golf is a good sport.

In brief, if it is a word which identifies anything you can see, hear, feel, taste, smell, or think about, it is a noun.

## B. The Pronoun

Doesn't the following sound silly?

Mr. Mall rose from Mr. Mall's chair to get Mr. Mall's evening paper. Mr. Mall usually had it brought to Mr. Mall, but Mr. Mall had sent Mr. Mall's family on a visit to Mr. Mall's brother.

This sounds better:

Mr. Mall rose from his chair to get his evening paper. He usually had it brought to him, but he had sent his family on a visit to his brother.

The improvement was brought about by the use of pronouns. "Pro" comes from the Latin and means "instead of," or "for." Thus pronouns are used instead of nouns. There are three kinds of pronouns.

1. **Personal**—used instead of names readily identified.

   > I, me, we, us
   > you
   > he, him, she, her, it, they, them

   Example: See paragraph above.

2. **Indefinite**—as the term suggests, used when no one in particular is meant, but one person at a time is being considered.

   > each, either, neither, one
   > somebody, everybody, nobody, anybody
   > some one, everyone, no one, anyone

   Example: **Everybody** is eating his lunch.

3. **Relative**—used to refer to people or things **and** to connect one part of a sentence to another.

   > (for people) who, whoever, whosoever, whom, whomever, whomsoever
   > (for things) which
   > (for either) that

   Examples: Tom is the one **whom** I called. (or **that**)
   The suit **which** I want is expensive. (or **that**)

## C. The Verb

The verb indicates what and when a noun or pronoun did something:

> The **lion** ROARED madly.

(Tells us what the lion—noun—did—at a previous date.)

or just makes a statement:

> We ARE very tired.

(Enables us to make a statement about "We"—pronoun—at this moment.)

The verb may consist of *one word*, as above:

> or two: I have eaten already.
> or three: They have been traveling.
> or four: By this time Sunday, I shall have been fishing for two hours.

The verb sometimes changes when the number changes:

> Singular (one person, place, or thing, etc.): George walks to work.
> Plural (2 or more people, places, or things, etc.): They walk every day.

The verb also has tense, or indicates time:

> Tomorrow (future): shall or will paint, have painted, have been painting.
> Today (present): paints, paint, am, is, are painting.
> Yesterday (past): painted, was, were painting, has, have, had painted, has, have, had been painting.

## D. The Adjective

If we had only the names for objects and people, our language would be dull, lack color and emotion. The adjective helps us get a better picture of a *noun or pronoun*. It may be directly attached to a word and influence its meaning:

I want a **large** piece of cake.
   (causes quantity to defeat manners)

She invited **only** me.
   (makes one exclusive)

or be separated from the word it influences by a verb:

That boy is **noisy**.
   (helps to warn one in advance)

The adjective may **merely describe**: tall man
or compare (**comparative degree**): taller than I
or select from 3 or more (**superlative degree**): **tallest** of the group

## E. The Adverb

Most frequently, the adverb gives us more information about a *verb*. That's why the "ad" syllable, meaning "toward, to," plus the "verb" is a very good definition in itself. Sometimes, however, the adverb may also describe an adjective or another adverb. Here are three examples:

1. Please tell the story **quickly**. ("tell" how?—information about a verb)
2. This table is **unusually** heavy. (how "heavy"?—information about an adjective)
3. She replied **rather** angrily. (how "angrily"?—information about an adverb)

The adverb may also **merely describe**: slowly
                        or **compare**: more slowly
                        or **select from 3 or more**: most slowly

There are other parts of speech, and books have been written on the principles of grammar that we have chosen *not* to discuss. But remember; we are interested in the subject only where it helps our spelling.

Certain helpful rules can be applied to words as they change from one part of speech to another. Study these rules carefully. Use them as further aids: Each shows how to BUILD THE WORD!

## 1. The "Y" Ending

When Y is preceded by a consonant, CHANGE Y TO I!

### a. Nouns: When the plural is formed—

country, countries     pantry, pantries
city, cities     baby, babies

### b. Verbs: When the tense changes—

try, tries, tried—BUT—trying (to avoid double I)
cry, cries, cried—BUT—crying (to avoid double I)
comply, complies, complied—BUT—complying (to avoid double I)
reply, replies, replied—BUT—replying (to avoid double I)

### c. Adjectives:

hearty, heartier, heartiest
lazy, lazier, laziest
cozy, cozier, coziest
busy, busier, busiest (also noun: business)

### d. Adverbs:

hearty, heartily     cozy, cozily
lazy, lazily     busy, busily

When Y is preceded by a vowel (a, e, i, o, u), KEEP the Y!

a. **Nouns:** When the plural is formed—

monkey, monkeys    donkey, donkeys
key, keys    alloy, alloys

b. **Verbs:** When the tense changes—

play, played, am playing, plays
survey, surveyed, was surveyed, surveys
lay, are laying, lays—BUT—laid, lain
slay, was slaying, slays—BUT—slain

c. **Adjectives and Adverbs:**

coy, coyly    boy, boyish, boyishly
cloy, cloying, cloyingly

d. **Two important exceptions:**

day, daily    gay, gaily

## 2. The Silent "E" Ending

Many words in the language end in E. Frequently, as in TAPE, SUPREME, KITE, ROPE, and USE, the letter is there to retain the "long" sound of the preceding vowel. At other times, there does not seem to be any good reason for its presence, as in SALVE, PROVE, SUITE, and LOVE, but it is there just the same. Because it only helps the sound of another letter, or is a useless remnant, it is called the SILENT VOWEL. When syllables are added to words ending in this silent E, special rules apply.

Example:

|  | |
|---|---|
| tribe | (silent E) |
| al | (syllable beginning with a vowel) |
| tribal | (THE SILENT E IS DROPPED WHEN A SYLLABLE BEGINNING WITH A VOWEL IS ADDED.) |

Example:

|  | |
|---|---|
| grieve | |
| ance | |
| grievance | (THE SILENT E IS DROPPED.) |

Try These:

| Word | Add | |
|---|---|---|
| skate | ing | _____ |
| blue | ish | _____ |
| advise | ing | _____ |
| | able | _____ |
| use | able | _____ |
| | age | _____ |
| | ing | _____ |
| console | ation | _____ |

**Answers:** skating, bluish, advising, advisable, usable, usage, using, consolation.

There are a few exceptions, but they are logical, so that you should remember them easily. If you have any trouble, fall back on the SEE-THINK-FEEL THE WORD treatment.

a. canoeing, hoeing—to avoid pronunciation difficulty, the E is retained. (also: shoe, toe)

b. dyeing, singeing—to avoid confusing them with **dying, singing,** the E is retained. (also: tinge)

c. CE and GE endings—to retain the sound of S in CE, and DJ in GE, the E is kept in the word. (serviceable, manageable, changeable, advantageous, courageous)

d. mileage—to avoid confusing it with **millage** (tax rate in mills per dollar) and to retain the long I sound, the E is kept.

The other part to this rule is not so reliable. When the silent E is followed by a syllable beginning with a consonant, the practice *generally* is to retain the E, as in GRATEFUL, LATELY, LAMENESS, ABATEMENT. There are numerous exceptions, however, and you are advised to check the individual words with a dictionary rather than depend on the rule. Watch out particularly for ARGUMENT, JUDGMENT, and ACKNOWLEDGMENT. And make sure you spell SINCERELY and NINETEEN correctly; they *do* follow the rule. Lastly, DEVELOPMENT has nothing to do with the rule at all since the original word is DEVELOP (no silent E ending)!

## 3. The "LY" Ending

The most frequent use of the LY syllable is to change adjectives into adverbs. When you are in doubt about the spelling of a word ending in LY:

a. Write the adjective form first.

b. Check the last letter.

If it is Y, treat it like any Y ending.

| | | |
|---|---|---|
| necessary | **Y to I** | necessarily |
| heavy | **Y to I** | heavily |

If it is LE, change E to Y and that's all!

| | | |
|---|---|---|
| considerable | **E to Y** | considerably |
| capable | **E to Y** | capably |

If it is L, leave it there!

| | | |
|---|---|---|
| usual | **L stays** | usually |
| oral | **L stays** | orally |

If it is E, leave it there!

| | | |
|---|---|---|
| extreme | **E stays** | extremely |
| late | **E stays** | lately |

Add LY to these:

| | | |
|---|---|---|
| satisfactory | _____ | definite | _____ |
| merry | _____ | absolute | _____ |
| happy | _____ | sincere | _____ |
| personal | _____ | able | _____ |
| natural | _____ | double | _____ |
| awful | _____ | subtle | _____ |

Answers: satisfactorily, merrily, happily, personally, naturally, awfully, definitely, absolutely, sincerely, ably, doubly, subtly.

## 4. The "ABLE-IBLE" Endings

This rule isn't foolproof. However, it will work 99% of the time. The occasional exception? Give it the treatment!

a. If you can form a word ending in IVE or SION, use IBLE.

| | |
|---|---|
| permission | permissible |
| divisive | divisible |
| resistive | resistible, irresistible |
| reversion | reversible |
| conversion | convertible |

b. If you cannot, use ABLE.

| | |
|---|---|
| depend | dependable |
| use | usable (silent E dropped) |
| sale | salable |
| receive | receivable |
| commend | commendable |

c. Here are two exceptions you can give the treatment at once:

| | |
|---|---|
| feasible | remittable |

## 5. The "C" Ending

Notice these two examples:

colic, colicky　　　picnic, picnicked, picnicking

The K is added before the final syllable to prevent the C's being sounded like an S.

Try it with these:

shellac, panic, traffic
(Add ING, ED, ER, or Y, if possible)

Answers: shellacking, shellacked, panicked, panicky, trafficking, trafficked.

## 6. The "FULL" Ending

In general, when you add this syllable to a word, omit one of the L's.

| | |
|---|---|
| hope, hopeful | skill, skillful, skilful |
| spite, spiteful | fate, fateful |

## 7. The "SEDE, CEED, CEDE" Endings

a. Only one word in the language uses S:
   superSede

b. Three words use CEED:
   proCEED, sucCEED, exCEED

c. All others use CEDE:

| | |
|---|---|
| reCEDE | preCEDE |
| conCEDE | interCEDE, etc. |

## 8. Unusual Plural Endings

a. "O"

If the singular form ends in an O preceded by a consonant, usually add ES.

| | |
|---|---|
| echo, echoes | potato, potatoes |
| Negro, Negroes | cargo, cargoes |

If the singular form ends in an O preceded by a vowel, always add only S.

| | |
|---|---|
| cameo, cameos | patio, patios |
| studio, studios | ratio, ratios |

**Also:**

musical terms—altos, sopranos
clipped words—photos, autos
recent words—gauchos, commandos

b. "Y"

We have already covered this:

Y preceded by a consonant, change Y to I, and add ES.
Y preceded by a vowel, add only S.

| | |
|---|---|
| puppy, puppies | relay, relays |
| berry, berries | convoy, convoys |

c. Irregular Nouns

Words taken from a foreign language often present problems. No general rules exist, so that each one must be checked with a dictionary. The best approach here, too, is the SEE-THINK-FEEL treatment.

hippopotamus, hippopotamuses, hippopotami
alumnus, alumni (male), alumna, alumnae (female)
phenomenon, phenomena

## 9. Front Syllables

So far we have been talking about spelling problems that are created by the addition of syllables at the ends of words. Many errors occur also at the beginnings, especially when the question of doubling a letter arises. You can handle these without trouble if you use this method:

a. Single Letter

**disappear**

A common misspelling of this word is to use an extra S. Here's what to do:

Separate the first syllable from the basic word:

**dis appear**

What does it end with? S.
What does the rest begin with? A.
Any double letter? NO!

**Again:**

   dis appoint       disappoint

Ends-S     Begins-A    Double? NO!

b. Double Letter

   misspell

Separate the first syllable from the basic word:

   mis spell

What does it end with? S.
What does the rest begin with? S.
Any double letter? YES! Double S.

**Again:**

   dis service       disservice

Ends-S     Begins-S    Double? YES!

**A few more of both kinds:**

| | |
|---|---|
| un necessary | unnecessary |
| re commend | recommend |
| dis approve | disapprove |
| a cross | across |
| ad dress | address |

## 10. Hyphenated Expressions

The tendency today is to use the hyphen (-) as little as possible. In fact, experts who prefer its use have been unable to agree on a set of rules. Therefore, when you aren't sure, leave out the hyphen. These are the preferred uses on which there is general agreement.

a. Fused Adjectives, Numbers
  i. Several words combined to form one adjective:
    never-to-be-forgotten day
    well-executed double play
  ii. Twenty-one, thirty-three, etc., up to ninety-nine

b. "Ex" and "Self"

When these syllables are attached to the beginning of a word, use the hyphen.

    ex-private     self-appointed     ex-counterman

c. Before a capital letter or a similar vowel

    un-American     re-echo
    pro-British      co-owner

## 11. The Apostrophe (')

This symbol is used in a variety of situations. If you omit a necessary apostrophe, you have misspelled the word, even though the error did not involve a letter.

a. To Indicate Possession, Ownership

This is its major use. Here, too, there is a lack of agreement among the experts. Fortunately, the easiest rule to apply also happens to be the most modern. Use this method and, if someone shows you another way, tell him you prefer to be up-to-date.

  i. If the word ends in S, use only (').

    Boys play games. I enjoy watching boys' games.
    Charles had a hat. Who took Charles' hat?
    Have you read Dickens' "A Tale of Two Cities"?

ii. If the word does **not** end in S, use ('S).

These are children's toys.
We looked for the girl's blue coat.
Ladies will exercise a lady's privilege.

iii. In groups of two or more, last member receives mark.

It's occupied by Chisholm and Boone's law firm.
I'm tired of every Tom, Dick, and Harry's complaint.

iv. In hyphenated expressions, place mark at end.

She visited her son-in-law's house.
Ask the sergeant-at-arms' permission.

v. Use mark on noun or pronoun attached to words ending in "ing." (No mark for personal pronouns)

They discussed **Cole's** leaving the force.
I wondered whether **someone else's** winning would upset her.
They didn't approve of **my** going.

**Important!** Remember these personal pronouns **never use the apostrophe!**

| | |
|---|---|
| mine, ours | yours |
| his, hers, its | theirs |
| whose | |

b. Plurals of Letters, Numbers, and Words Used As Words

How many "r's" does the word have?
There are three 2's in my number.
The company's president used too many "and's" in his speech.

c. Contractions:
See Chapter V, p. 33.

## 12. Capital Letters

Good spelling habits require that you use these carefully.

a. Titles of Books, Plays, Articles, Newspapers, Magazines, etc.

The first and last words of a title are always written with capital letters. In the rest, only articles (a, an, the), prepositions (of, by, to), and conjunctions (and, if, as), when they are shorter than four letters, may be written without capitals.

> The Taming of the Shrew
> The Shape of Things to Come
> What Men Live By

b. Proper Nouns

Any word that becomes the name of a particular place, person, or thing should be capitalized. Very often, the same word may be either proper or common.

**Observe:**

> He bought a piece of **territory** in the **northwest** part of the state.
> The establishment of the **Northwest Territory** raised controversial issues.
> People who live in the **north** frequently go to the **south** in the winter.
> The Civil War involved the **North** against the **South**.

**Note:**

When a proper noun becomes an adjective, the capital letter is retained.

> France is the place to study **French** customs.

If you plan to travel to South America, learn the **Spanish** language.

It was a wallop of **Ruthian** proportions.

c. **First Words**

**Lines of Poetry**

"Take her up tenderly,
Lift her with care,
Fashioned so slenderly,
Young and so fair."

**Direct Quotations**

"Off with her head!" shouted Henry.
Henry shouted, "Off with her head!"

**Salutations, Closings of Letters**

Dear Mr. Smith:
Sincerely yours,

Rewrite the following, inserting all capital letters that have been left out:

72 ellen drive
rockaway, new jersey
january 6, 1954

dear john,

when i spoke to you about "south pacific" i didn't realize that your french cousin had expressed a desire to go, too. well, as shakespeare said,

"let me not to the marriage of true minds
admit impediments"

in this case i'll be preacher jones, and perform the ceremony of wedding broadway to gallic charm.

cordially,
horton

Now check:

> 72 Ellen Drive
> Rockaway, New Jersey
> January 6, 1954

Dear John,

When I spoke to you about "South Pacific" I didn't realize that your French cousin had expressed a desire to go, too. Well, as Shakespeare said,

"Let me not to the marriage of true minds
Admit impediments"

In this case I'll be Preacher Jones and perform the ceremony of wedding Broadway to Gallic charm.

> Cordially,
> Horton

The review paragraphs in this chapter will contain samplings, rather than the complete list of words used as illustration. You understand, of course, that the main stress was on rules rather than on individual words. Your knowledge of these (and some exceptions) is what we want to test.

## Special Endings

Willie almost **cried** when he came face to face with the monkeys. For some reason, they reminded him of furry babies, but the way they **lazily surveyed** him made him feel sure they were very old. Suddenly, Uncle Jasper invited Willie to go **canoeing**. It was a **commendable** suggestion meant to keep the boy **manageable**. However, it was going to be **extremely** difficult to start the trip **happily** because at the moment tears seemed **irresistible**. Suddenly again, two astounding **phenomena interceded** in **panicky** Willie's behalf. First, a group of **sopranos,** sitting in a **convertible,** drove by, singing "Lonesome **Cargoes."** Then, a **tribal** chieftain, wearing a string of **cameos, skillfully** began leading two **hippopotamuses** into a dance. So **advantageous** was this welcome change that Willie allowed a **grateful** grin to **supersede** his **boyishly** sad expression. Then Willie woke up. It had been a dreadful nightmare.

### Front Syllables, Hyphens, Apostrophes

What is meant by the term **"un-American"?** Well, **it's** many things. One who **disapproves** of **everyone's** right to speak freely is offering a **disservice** to his country. The **self-appointed** critic of **another's** beliefs acts **unpatriotically** when he **recommends** that even a **person's** thinking should be controlled. Abraham Lincoln, in several **addresses,** spoke of the need for **well-developed** citizens from **twenty-one** to **seventy-one** who would become **co-owners** of a country that accepted every **Tom, Dick,** and **Harry's** differences, allowed no **"anti's"** to develop against any group, and used the three **"r's"** to be watchful of your interests and **theirs.** In this way, fearing some **so-called** strong man would become **unnecessary. Unable** to make headway, such an individual would quickly learn that a **dictator's** hand could not reach **across** the land without its being broken.

In the foregoing paragraphs there are fifty key words. If you miss any, go back and study the rules which apply to your error.

_____

_____

_____

_____

_____

_____

_____

_____

The last two chapters have thrown rules at you by the handful. Perhaps by now you wish you had skipped them. There are so many things to remember.

It isn't really that bad. Bear in mind that the majority of words cannot be classified. They require individual study. You know how to do that. If you prefer to use the SEE-THINK-FEEL method for all words, fine! Any rule that *bothers you* isn't worth *bothering with*. If you can remember the rule easily, and it helps, use it. If you can't, forget the rule and treat each word by itself.

## · VII ·

## The Treatment

## Six Minutes A Day!

It's time to take stock. You now know the basic system which can be *applied to any word:*

### SEE THE WORD!

Get a picture in your mind, especially of the difficult part of the word.

### THINK THE WORD!

Prepare some bit of easily-remembered nonsense for the troublesome syllable or letter.

### FEEL THE WORD!

Trace the word WITH YOUR FINGER, and learn to write it while concentrating on something else.

You are also familiar with the devices for handling large groups of words:

### SAY THE WORD!

Be careful not to leave out, add, or confuse syllables and letters. Use other words in the same family to locate key vowels in words. Be careful of words that sound alike. Learn the ACCENTED SYLLABLE RULE! FSA!

BUILD THE WORD!

Follow the changes in spelling from one part of speech to another. Study unusual plurals, front and back syllables, hyphens, possessives, and capital letters.

These are the five simple steps we mentioned in the first chapter. Together they are the tested way to make the correct spelling of any word a lifelong habit. Now we are going to prescribe a simple six minute a day program to make sure that good spelling stays with you forever.

## DAILY PROGRAM

| Time | Procedure |
|------|-----------|
| MORNING | A. Look up the pronunciation of your troublesome word in a good dictionary. |
| 3 Minutes | SAY THE WORD. Then observe how it is built. |
| | Set up the image to SEE THE WORD. |
| | Stare at it for ten seconds. Look away at another surface. Count five; "see" the image with your mind. Write the word rapidly. (90 seconds) |
| | B. Prepare the BOND. |
| | THINK THE WORD. |
| | Write the word as you think of the association. (30 seconds) |

C. Write the word in large script letters.

FEEL THE WORD by tracing it three times with your finger.

Say each letter aloud as you trace.

Write the word rapidly, and, as you do, say anything that comes into your mind, or repeat the association. (60 seconds)

AFTERNOON

Repeat the entire procedure outlined above, except for looking the word up in the dictionary.

1 Minute, 30 seconds

This should take about half the time it took you in the morning since you are simply recalling what you have done.

Do not skip any steps. It will require patience, but stay with it.

EVENING

Repeat everything once more.

1 Minute, 30 seconds

Don't try more than ONE WORD A DAY.

Anything more will divide your attention, and reduce the single effect you want to establish.

With this plan you can cover five words from Monday to Friday. Use the week end for review by preparing a few sentences or a paragraph which contains the words you studied that week. Ask someone to dictate the material, if possible.

In the next chapter you will find a ninety day trial which uses the six minute a day routine so, before you go ahead, make certain you understand this simple program.

# VIII

# Ninety Day Trial

No one gets to be a good golfer simply by listening to a professional, nor, for that matter, simply by reading a book. By itself the best instruction in the world does not substantially improve a student's skill. The difference between the person who "knows how" and the person who "can do" is quite obviously practice, practice, and more practice. This is as true of spelling as it is of golf, or tennis, or bridge, or learning to play the piano.

Strangely enough, moreover, spelling is one of the few fields where practice really *does* make perfect . . . and where perfection is the only thing that counts. For example, if you sink nine putts out of ten in golf you are considered an extraordinarily good golfer. But in spelling you don't win any prizes for getting nine letters right in a ten letter word. You either spell a word perfectly or you misspell it. There is no comparative degree in the game of spelling.

What follows therefore is a practice session. It is also a ninety day trial by which you can prove to yourself that good spellers are made, not born.

Ninety days may sound like a long stretch, but actually the total time you'll have to devote to practice equals only nine hours or slightly more than one working day. It is little enough to ask when you consider the goal: to make you a perfect speller.

The practice list for the ninety day trial consists of sixty words. These so-called demons are not particularly unusual or difficult, but they are commonly misspelled by more than 25% of educated people.

You may already know how to spell some of the words. If you do, cross out the ones that have been offered and write in the substitutes you have chosen from the lists provided in the appendix. The individual words are important, but the most important thing is the steady, planned attack. Because once you've become experienced, *any* spelling demon can be tamed by giving it the treatment.

Take one word a day and spend six minutes on it. Study each exactly as described in "THE TREATMENT." Cover five words a week. Use Saturdays and Sundays for review. At the end of each month, do the test on the month's twenty words. If you miss any, don't go ahead until your score is 100%.

**Here are seven important suggestions which will help you start on the right road:**

1. Before you proceed with a word, check its pronunciation in a dictionary, **even if you think you know it**; then write it in pencil in the space provided on each page that follows. I have deliberately omitted this information so that you will train yourself to use the dictionary often as the final authority on the spoken word.

2. Use the spaces under "Image" for additional diagrams you may think of, under "Bond" for further nonsense associations, and under "Trace" for writing the word in script during the daily review. **Your own handwriting should form** the basis for the tracing practice.

3. Use the fifteen sentences for the week-end reviews. Take ten (two for each word) on Saturday, and five (one for each word) on Sunday. Have someone dictate them, or glance rapidly at each, memorize it, and then write it.

4. A notation like "VI—Front Syllables" refers to the rule or suggestion covered in the chapter indicated by the Roman numeral. Review the section as you practice.

5. If possible, form a team with another person working on spelling. Help each other by exchanging dictation of test paragraphs and sentences. Write weekly letters in which you purposely use newly-learned words.

6. Do not assume that you need peace and quiet for your practice sessions. Train yourself to concentrate even in the midst of great noise and confusion. Make your spelling automatic!

7. Before you start be sure you understand and can apply the techniques discussed in previous chapters. Also be certain you can follow the six minute a day program. Once you do start, don't let yourself give up. Be serious. Be faithful. Six minutes each day. That's all.

FIRST WEEK:     Monday
Word 1:             co op er a tion

Pronunciation:  _____

Image:              COOPeration
  See A,
  page 67          _____

                       _____

                       _____

Bond:                 I need your COOPeration to clean the
  See B,            COOP.
  page 67              See VI—Front Syllables

                       _____

                       _____

                       _____

Trace:              *cooperation*
  See C,
  page 68          _____

                       _____

                       _____

Sentences:         **Cooperation** among nations will lead to
                       peace.
                       I offer my **cooperation** gladly.
                       A good team depends upon **cooperation**.

FIRST WEEK:   Tuesday
Word 2:   ac quaint ance

Pronunciation:  _____

Image:   acQUAINTAnce

_____

_____

_____

Bond:   He speaks with a QUAINT A.

_____

_____

_____

Trace:   *acquaintance*

_____

_____

_____

Sentences:   My **acquaintance** is coming to see me.
Give me an **acquaintance,** and I'll make him a friend.
A smile and a greeting can make an **acquaintance.**

**FIRST WEEK:** Wednesday
**Word 3:** gov ern ment

Pronunciation: _____

Image: goVERNment

_____

_____

_____

Bond: VERN Porter works for the goVERN-
ment.
See V—Omitted Syllables

_____

_____

_____

Trace: *government*

_____

_____

_____

Sentences: **Government** separates men from beasts.
Only a weak **government** permits in-
flation.
Your ballot helps you control your **government**.

**FIRST WEEK:**    Thursday
**Word 4:**    re quire ment

**Pronunciation:** _____

**Image:**    reQUIREment

_____

_____

_____

**Bond:**
     A QUIRE of paper will meet my reQUIREment.
     See VI—Silent "E" Ending

_____

_____

_____

**Trace:**    *requirement*

_____

_____

_____

**Sentences:**
     One **requirement** is a local address.
     If you meet the **requirement**, you will be accepted.
     No one is permitted to ignore a **requirement**.

FIRST WEEK:     Friday
Word 5:          ex cel lent

Pronunciation:   _____

Image:           exCELLEnt

                 _____

                 _____

                 _____

Bond:            The prisoner in CELL E shows ex-
                 CELLEnt conduct.

                 _____

                 _____

                 _____

Trace:           *excellent*

                 _____

                 _____

                 _____

Sentences:       **Excellent** apples can be bought now.
                 She has an **excellent** program arranged
                 for us.
                 The fishing in this lake is **excellent**.

Review: 10 Sentences on Saturday

_____

_____

_____

_____

_____

_____

_____

_____

_____

_____

5 Sentences on Sunday

_____

_____

_____

_____

_____

SECOND WEEK: Monday

Word 6:           def i nite

Pronunciation:    _____

Image:            defInIte

                  _____

                  _____

                  _____

Bond:             An I for an I is a defInIte Biblical
                  saying.

                  _____

                  _____

                  _____

Trace:            _____ *definite* _____

                  _____

                  _____

                  _____

Sentences:        **Definite** signs of spring are here.
                  Give me a **definite** answer, please.
                  He could not make the time **definite**.

SECOND WEEK: Tuesday
Word 7:         cat a log

Pronunciation:  _____

Image:          catALOG

                _____

                _____

                _____

Bond:           You will find even A LOG for sale in
                the catALOG.

                _____

                _____

                _____

Trace:          _____ *catalog* _____

                _____

                _____

                _____

Sentences:      **Catalog** these prices for the next issue.
                You will find this **catalog** in many Amer-
                ican homes.
                Let's take a look in the **catalog**.

**SECOND WEEK:** Wednesday
Word 8:        sense

Pronunciation:        _____

Image:        seNSe

        _____
        _____
        _____

Bond:        NS means "no seNSe."

        _____
        _____
        _____

Trace:        *sense*

        _____
        _____
        _____

Sentences:        **Sense** comes with experience.
        He could **sense** the coming storm.
        Avoid accidents by using common **sense**.

**SECOND WEEK:** **Thursday**
Word 9:  bul le tin

Pronunciation:  _____

Image:  BULLETIN

_____

_____

_____

Bond:  The BULLET lodged IN the BULLE-
TIN board.

_____

_____

_____

Trace:  _____ *bulletin* _____

_____

_____

_____

Sentences:  Bulletin 9 will be issued on Monday.
This is a **bulletin** from the front.
Tack this on the **bulletin** board.

**SECOND WEEK:** Friday
Word 10:     oc ca sion

Pronunciation:     _____

Image:     oCCasion

_____

_____

_____

Bond:     A 2 CC dose will do for this oCCasion.

_____

_____

_____

Trace:     *occasion*

_____

_____

_____

Sentences:     An **occasion** like this will be long re-
membered.
Let me take this **occasion** to thank you.
I'm sure it will be a great **occasion**.

Review: 10 Sentences on Saturday

_____

_____

_____

_____

_____

_____

_____

_____

_____

_____

5 Sentences on Sunday

_____

_____

_____

_____

_____

**THIRD WEEK:** Monday
Word 11: rec om men da tion

Pronunciation: _____

Image: reCoMMendation

_____

_____

_____

Bond: I C the MM's in reCoMMendation.
See VI—Front Syllables

_____

_____

_____

Trace: *recommendation*

_____

_____

_____

Sentences: **Recommendation** is essential for a job.
I shall give my **recommendation** when
it is asked.
Send in your **recommendation**.

THIRD WEEK: Tuesday
Word 12: fi nan cial

Pronunciation: _____

Image: fINANcial

_____

_____

_____

Bond: FINANcial success begins IN AN account with a bank.

_____

_____

_____

Trace: *financial*

_____

_____

_____

Sentences: Financial news is found in most newspapers.

What is the financial rating of this company?

The nature of this report is financial.

THIRD WEEK: Wednesday
Word 13: de ter mine

Pronunciation: _____

Image: deterMINE

_____

_____

_____

Bond: MINE will deterMINE the final result.

_____

_____

_____

Trace: *determine*

_____

_____

_____

Sentences: **Determine** the answer by dividing.
When did he **determine** to follow this policy?
I wish I knew what the fates will **determine**.

**THIRD WEEK:** Thursday
Word 14: nec es sar y

Pronunciation: _____

Image: neCESSary

_____

_____

_____

Bond: It is neCESSary to keep a CESS pool clean.

_____

_____

_____

Trace: _necessary_

_____

_____

_____

Sentences: **Necessary** steps are being taken.
It won't be **necessary** for you to come.
I wonder whether that was **necessary**.

THIRD WEEK: Friday
Word 15: quan ti ty

Pronunciation: _____

Image: quANTITY

_____

_____

_____

Bond: A quANTITY of ants might be called an ANTITY.

_____

_____

_____

Trace: *quantity*

_____

_____

_____

Sentences: **Quantity** is what we need now.
The same **quantity** sold for less.
I want a greater **quantity**.

Review: 10 Sentences on Saturday

_____

_____

_____

_____

_____

_____

_____

_____

_____

_____

5 Sentences on Sunday

_____

_____

_____

_____

_____

FOURTH WEEK: Monday
Word 16: con science

Pronunciation: _____

Image: conSCIENCE

_____

_____

_____

Bond: CON plus SCIENCE equals CON-
SCIENCE.

_____

_____

_____

Trace: *conscience*

_____

_____

_____

Sentences: "**Conscience** makes cowards of us all."
Let your **conscience** be your guide.
He knew this would not satisfy his
**conscience**.

FOURTH WEEK: Tuesday
Word 17: au thor i ty

Pronunciation: _____

Image: auTHORity

_____

_____

_____

Bond: The god THOR was an ancient symbol of auTHORity.

_____

_____

_____

Trace: *authority*

_____

_____

_____

Sentences: Authority should rest with the wise and
just.
You have no authority to do that.
You will have to state your authority.

FOURTH WEEK: Wednesday

Word 18:        ben e fit

Pronunciation:        _____

Image:        benEFit

        _____

        _____

        _____

Bond:        Sound and spell the EF in benEFit.

        _____

        _____

        _____

Trace:        *benefit*

        _____

        _____

        _____

Sentences:        **Benefit** yourself by checking the value.
        Of what **benefit** will this be?
        His major interest was the public **bene-fit.**

**FOURTH WEEK:** Thursday
Word 19: ba sis

Pronunciation: _____

Image: baSIS

_____

_____

_____

Bond: Billy was punished on the baSIS of what
SIS said.

_____

_____

_____

Trace: *basis*

_____

_____

_____

Sentences: The **basis** for his action was the report.
You have no **basis** for your complaint.
The loan will require a sound **basis.**

**FOURTH WEEK:** Friday

Word 20: ex ist ence

Pronunciation: _____

Image: exisTENce

_____

_____

_____

Bond: This firm has been in exisTENce for TEN years.

_____

_____

_____

Trace: *existence*

_____

_____

_____

Sentences: **Existence** is the first desire of mankind.
I did not know of the **existence** of this product.
How long has it been in **existence?**

Review: 15 Sentences on Saturday

_____

_____

_____

_____

_____

_____

_____

1 Paragraph (next page)
Sunday Morning

_____

_____

1 Paragraph Sunday Evening

_____

_____

_____

_____

Review Paragraphs: First Month

Each paragraph covers words 1-20. If you miss any in the first, study them carefully, one a day in the regular way; then try the second paragraph.

I.

If we were to catalog the requirements of good government, we would list certain definite points. There would have to be one person in authority whose good sense would inspire cooperation on every occasion. He would handle a bulletin from abroad with the same clear conscience as he would a financial problem at home. No mere acquaintance would be able to benefit on the basis of friendship, nor would a party recommendation be necessary to determine fitness for office. Unfortunately there is no great quantity of such excellent men in existence.

II.

The existence of the mail order catalog has been of benefit to many people for years. Government workers, whose financial position is never among the highest, can buy necessary items at fair prices because the basis on which these companies operate is quantity sales, excellent materials, and low profit requirements. To determine the definite aid this type of selling is to others as well, one may read the recommendations that appear in bulletins issued by consumer organizations whose authority and cooperation are sought by persons of good sense all over the country. On one occasion, an acquaintance of mine remarked that the public conscience made business through the mails possible.

**FIFTH WEEK:** Monday

**Word 21:** per ma nent

Pronunciation: _____

Image: perMANEnt

_____

_____

_____

Bond: The MANE is a perMANEnt part of a lion.

_____

_____

_____

Trace: *permanent*

_____

_____

_____

Sentences: **Permanent** plans were made.

This is a **permanent** part of the build-ing.

This time we'll make it **permanent**.

**FIFTH WEEK:**  Tuesday
**Word 22:**  ac com mo date

Pronunciation: _____

Image:  aCCoMModate

_____

_____

_____

Bond:  "The Double C-Modern Motel" We aCCoMModate 50 guests.

_____

_____

_____

Trace:  *accommodate*

_____

_____

_____

Sentences:  **Accommodate** me by changing this bill, please.

We cannot **accommodate** you before Monday.

How many do you think they will **accommodate**?

**FIFTH WEEK:** Wednesday
**Word 23:** ex ten sion

Pronunciation: _____

Image: exTENSion

_____

_____

_____

Bond: The exTENSion will cost TENS of thousands.

_____

_____

_____

Trace: *extension*

_____

_____

_____

_____

Sentences: **Extension** of your credit is not possible.
I shall need the **extension** for an extra bedroom.
What is the number of the **extension**?

**FIFTH WEEK:** Thursday
**Word 24:** mis chief

Pronunciation: _____

Image: misCHIEF

_____

_____

_____

Bond: He was the CHIEF cause of the mis-CHIEF.

_____

_____

_____

Trace: *mischief*

_____

_____

_____

Sentences: **Mischief** is common to small boys.
It was the kind of **mischief** that had to be stopped.
Now don't you get into any **mischief**.

FIFTH WEEK:    Friday
Word 25:    A mer i can

Pronunciation:    _____

Image:    AmERICan

_____

_____

_____

Bond:    ERIC is now an AmERICan.

_____

_____

Trace:    _American_

_____

_____

_____

Sentences:    **American** ideals are founded on freedom.

He is an **American** by birth.

To be selfish is to be un-**American**.

Review: 10 Sentences on Saturday

_____

_____

_____

_____

_____

_____

_____

_____

_____

5 Sentences on Sunday

_____

_____

_____

_____

**SIXTH WEEK:** Monday
**Word 26:** ex ec u tive

Pronunciation: _____

Image: exeCUTive

_____

_____

_____

Bond: The exeCUTive got a CUT on his arm.

_____

_____

_____

Trace: _____ *executive* _____

_____

_____

_____

Sentences: **Executive** talent is a rare thing.
He is an **executive** for a large company.
That's the name of the new **executive**.

**SIXTH WEEK:** Tuesday
Word 27: thor ough

Pronunciation: _____

Image: thoROUGH

_____

_____

_____

Bond: It was a ROUGH but thoROUGH job.

_____

_____

_____

Trace: ___ *thorough* ___

_____

_____

_____

Sentences: **Thorough** work is necessary in science.
It was a **thorough** success from the be-
ginning.
That report seems to be very **thorough**.

**SIXTH WEEK:** Wednesday
Word 28: par tial

Pronunciation: _____

Image: PARTial

_____

_____

_____

bond: A PART is a PARTial amount.

_____

_____

_____

Trace: *partial*

_____

_____

_____

Sentences: **Partial** payment is not enough.
Try not to be **partial** in your attitude.
The score shows that you have a **par-tial**.

**SIXTH WEEK:** Thursday
Word 29: bas ket ball

Pronunciation: _____

Image: BASKETball

_____

_____

_____

Bond: A BASKET and a BALL are the tools of BASKETball.

_____

_____

_____

Trace: *basketball*

_____

_____

_____

Sentences: Basketball is an American game.
He plays basketball in the winter.
I went to see a game of basketball.

**SIXTH WEEK:** Friday
Word 30: judg ment

Pronunciation: _____

Image: judGMent

_____

_____

_____

Bond: Good judGMent is found in Good Men.

_____

_____

_____

Trace: *judgment*

_____

_____

_____

Sentences: **Judgment** was pronounced the follow-
ing day.
He used his **judgment** in deciding.
This will need careful **judgment**.

Review: 10 Sentences on Saturday

_____

_____

_____

_____

_____

_____

_____

_____

_____

_____

5 Sentences on Sunday

_____

_____

_____

_____

_____

**SEVENTH WEEK:  Monday**
Word 31:        ca pac i ty

Pronunciation:  _____

Image:          capaCITY

                _____

                _____

                _____

Bond:           The CITY was filled to capaCITY.

                _____

                _____

                _____

Trace:          *capacity*

                _____

                _____

                _____

Sentences:      **Capacity** business was being done.
                What is the **capacity** of the room?
                We ought to know the **capacity**.

**SEVENTH WEEK:** Tuesday

**Word 32:**   war rant

**Pronunciation:** _____

**Image:**   WARRANt

_____

_____

_____

**Bond:**   During the WAR he RAN from a WAR-RANt officer.

_____

_____

_____

**Trace:**   _warrant_

_____

_____

_____

**Sentences:**   A warrant for his arrest was issued.
Do you warrant the contents of thi
product?
I cannot honor this warrant.

**SEVENTH WEEK:** Wednesday
Word 33:      lit er a ture

Pronunciation: _____

Image:        litERAture

_____

_____

_____

Bond:         This ERA has produced good litERA-
              ture.

_____

_____

_____

Trace:        *literature*

_____

_____

_____

Sentences:    **Literature** delights the mind.
              The study of **literature** is required in
              college.
              Every war produces its own **literature**.

SEVENTH WEEK: Thursday
Word 34: crit i cism

Pronunciation: _____

Image: CRITICism

_____

_____

_____

Bond: A CRITIC offers CRITICism.

_____

_____

_____

Trace: *criticism*

_____

_____

_____

Sentences: **Criticism** can promote growth.
Do not accept **criticism** from the unin-
formed.
He conducts a column of dramatic
**criticism**.

**SEVENTH WEEK:** Friday
Word 35: in ter rupt

Pronunciation: _____

Image: intERRupt

_____

_____

_____

Bond: You ERR when you intERRupt.

_____

_____

_____

Trace: *interrupt*

_____

_____

_____

Sentences: **Interrupt** me when the time is up.
If you **interrupt** him he will become angry.
I don't think they should **interrupt**.

Review: 10 Sentences on Saturday

_____

_____

_____

_____

_____

_____

_____

_____

_____

_____

5 Sentences on Sunday

_____

_____

_____

_____

_____

**EIGHTH WEEK:** Monday

Word 36:      zo ol o gy

Pronunciation:  _____

Image:        ZOOlogy

_____

_____

_____

Bond:         Study ZOOlogy in a ZOO.
              See VI—Front Syllables

_____

_____

_____

Trace:        _____*zoology*_____

_____

_____

_____

Sentences:    **Zoology** is the science of animal life.
              A course in **zoology** will be given this
              fall.
              "Zoo" comes from the first syllable of
              **zoology**.

**EIGHTH WEEK: Tuesday**
Word 37:          as cer tain

Pronunciation: _____

Image:          asCERTAIN

_____

_____

_____

Bond:           When you ASCERTAIN you become
                AS CERTAIN as possible.

_____

_____

_____

Trace:          _ascertain_

_____

_____

_____

Sentences:      **Ascertain** the truth of the statement.
                I cannot **ascertain** the real reason.
                This is something I must **ascertain**.

**EIGHTH WEEK:** Wednesday

Word 38: trea son

Pronunciation: _____

Image: tREASON

_____

_____

_____

Bond: There is no good REASON for tREA-
SON.

_____

_____

_____

Trace: _treason_

_____

_____

_____

Sentences: Treason can be punished by death.
"If this be treason, make the most of it."
Selling official information is an act of
treason.

**EIGHTH WEEK:** Thursday

Word 39: ex haust ed

Pronunciation: _____

Image: exHAUSted

_____

_____

_____

Bond: **HA, you have not ex HAUSted US.**

_____

_____

_____

Trace: _exhausted_

_____

_____

_____

Sentences: **Exhausted**, he just sat there.
You have **exhausted** me, my boy.
That comedian leaves me **exhausted**.

**EIGHTH WEEK:** Friday
Word 40:    dor mi to ry

Pronunciation:    _____

Image:    dORMITOry

_____

_____

_____

Bond:    Mrs. ORMITO ran the dORMITOry.

_____

_____

_____

Trace:    _____ *dormitory* _____

_____

_____

_____

Sentences:    **Dormitory** rules were very strict.
This is the **dormitory** for men.
The party took place in the **dormitory**.

Review: 15 Sentences on Saturday

_____

_____

_____

_____

_____

_____

    1 Paragraph (next page)
     Sunday Morning

_____

_____

_____

    1 Paragraph Sunday Evening

_____

_____

_____

_____

Review Paragraphs: Second Month

The first paragraph covers words 21-40. The second offers you another look at 1-20. Should you miss any, be sure to go over them again (as if they were new words) before you continue with the next set.

I.

It took a **basketball** scandal to awaken the **American** public to the fact that **mischief** can be spread in any **dormitory**. It is easy to hurl **criticism** at officials who lacked good **judgment**, or even at the high **executive** who was blind to the **treason** being committed under his very nose. However, the **permanent** cure is not to be found in an **extension** of the investigation but in a **thorough** return to the real purpose of education. The **exhausted** rooter should be taught that his **capacity** for wise living and his ability to **ascertain** how he can fit the needs of society will best be developed by the study of subjects like **literature**, history, **mathematics**, and **zoology** than by the size of the score of his favorite team. Sports should not **interrupt** the basic program, but should become a **partial** relief from the daily grind. Let the desire to **accommodate** the athletic hero not lead to a **warrant** for his arrest on charges of bribery.

II.

A **bulletin** from the **financial** division announced that a **government** order would make it **necessary** to **determine** more carefully the **quantity** of goods that could be listed in the **catalog**. Since the new **requirement** set **definite** limits, a **recommendation** was made that full **cooperation** be the **basis** for future action. In one **sense** the **existence** of the regulation gave the company an **excellent** chance to make its **acquaint-**

ance with those products that would benefit both the consumer and the seller. No one in good conscience would take the authority on this occasion to ignore the report, but would proceed to make the proper adjustments.

### Write Words Incorrectly Spelled Below:

_____

_____

_____

_____

_____

### Compose Paragraph After Study of Missed Words:

_____

_____

_____

_____

_____

**NINTH WEEK:** Monday
**Word 41:** guard i an

Pronunciation: _____

Image: GUARDian

_____

_____

_____

Bond:      The GUARDian will GUARD my interests.

_____

_____

_____

Trace: _____ *guardian* _____

_____

_____

_____

Sentences:      **Guardian** rights were given to his uncle.
Refer this to the **guardian** for proper action.
I think we ought to ask her **guardian**.

NINTH WEEK: Tuesday
Word 42: du ly

Pronunciation: _____

Image: dULY

_____

_____

_____


Bond: The note was dULY paid in JULY.

_____

_____

_____


Trace: *duly*

_____

_____

_____


Sentences: **Duly** signed statements were mailed.
The message has **duly** arrived.
The bill must be paid **duly**.

| | |
|---|---|
| **NINTH WEEK:** | Wednesday |
| **Word 43:** | sov er eign |

Pronunciation: _____

Image: soveREIGN

_____

_____

_____

Bond: The REIGN of the soveREIGN was short.

_____

_____

_____

Trace: *sovereign*

_____

_____

_____

Sentences: **Sovereign** rights were given the ruler.
He has been the **sovereign** for forty years.
The boy dreamed that one day he would be **sovereign**.

**NINTH WEEK:** Thursday
**Word 44:** peas ant

**Pronunciation:** _____

**Image:** PEASant

_____

_____

_____

**Bond:** A PEASant sometimes ate only PEAS.

_____

_____

_____

**Trace:** _peasant_

_____

_____

_____

**Sentences:**  **Peasant** rights were simply unknown.
It was the **peasant** who longed for a revolt.
The salt tax was a heavy burden on the **peasant**.

**NINTH WEEK:** Friday
**Word 45:** ex traor di nar y

Pronunciation: _____

Image: EXTRAordinary

_____

_____

_____

Bond:     EXTRAordinary means something EX-
TRA above ORDINARY.

_____

_____

_____

Trace: *extraordinary*

_____

_____

_____

Sentences:     **Extraordinary** events were taking place.
    It was an **extraordinary** exhibition of
skill.
    It is nothing **extraordinary**.

Review: 10 Sentences on Saturday

_____

_____

_____

_____

_____

_____

_____

_____

_____

_____

5 Sentences on Sunday

_____

_____

_____

_____

_____

**TENTH WEEK:** Monday
Word 46:          mon arch y

Pronunciation:    _____

Image:            monARCHy

                  _____

                  _____

                  _____

Bond:             The ARCH was a symbol of the mon-
                  ARCHy.

                  _____

                  _____

                  _____

Trace:            _____ *monarchy* _____

                  _____

                  _____

                  _____

Sentences:        A **monarchy** will not be established.
                  The aim of the **monarchy** was to create
                  order.
                  The people voted against the **monarchy**.

**TENTH WEEK:** Tuesday
Word 47:        cor dial ly

Pronunciation:        _____

Image:        cordiALLY

        _____

        _____

        _____

Bond:        His ALLY replied cordiALLY.
        See VI—the "LY" Ending

        _____

        _____

        _____

Trace:        *cordially*

        _____

        _____

        _____

Sentences:        **Cordially** was hardly the way he spoke.
        They were **cordially** given answers.
        Everyone was received **cordially**.

**TENTH WEEK:** Wednesday
Word 48:     mir a cle

Pronunciation:     _____

Image:     mIRAcle

    _____

    _____

    _____

Bond:     IRA thought it was a mIRAcle.
    See V—Word Relatives

    _____

    _____

    _____

Trace:     _____ *miracle* _____

    _____

    _____

    _____

Sentences:     **"Miracle** power" is an advertising slogan.
    It seemed that a **miracle** was about to
    happen.
    He would be saved only by a **miracle**.

**TENTH WEEK:** Thursday
Word 49:       clothes

Pronunciation:      _____

Image:            CLOTHes

                     _____

                     _____

                     _____

Bond:           There is CLOTH in CLOTHes.

                     _____

                     _____

                     _____

Trace:          _____ _clothes_ _____

                     _____

                     _____

                     _____

Sentences:      **Clothes** make the man.
               You will need warm **clothes** in this cli-
               mate.
               His business was to press **clothes.**

| TENTH WEEK: | Friday |
|---|---|
| Word 50: | pri or |

Pronunciation: _____

Image: pRIOr

_____

_____

_____

Bond:     They stopped pRIOr to reaching the RIO Grande.

_____

_____

_____

Trace:     *prior*

_____

_____

_____

Sentences:     **Prior** to his speech, the chairman asked for applause.
    It happened **prior** to my arrival.
    I don't know whose rights are **prior**.

Review: 10 Sentences on Saturday

_____

_____

_____

_____

_____

_____

_____

_____

_____

_____

5 Sentences on Sunday

_____

_____

_____

_____

_____

**ELEVENTH WEEK: Monday**

Word 51:      com mit tee

Pronunciation:     _____

Image:     coMMiTTEE

_____

_____

_____

Bond:     Double MTE when you write coMMiT-TEE.

_____

_____

_____

Trace:     _committee_

_____

_____

_____

Sentences:     **Committee** members must be present.
Give it to the **committee** for further action.
Who is the head of the **committee**?

**ELEVENTH WEEK: Tuesday**

Word 52:          cour te sy

Pronunciation:    _____

Image:            COURTesy

                  _____

                  _____

                  _____

Bond:             COURTesy was part of COURT man-
                  ners.

                  _____

                  _____

                  _____

Trace:            _____*courtesy*_____

                  _____

                  _____

                  _____

Sentences:        **Courtesy** is a way of life.
                  An act of **courtesy** is always admired.
                  The children must be taught **courtesy**.

**ELEVENTH WEEK:** Wednesday

Word 53:        o rig i nal

Pronunciation:        _____

Image:        oriGINal

_____

_____

_____

Bond:        It was a model of the oriGINal cotton GIN.
        See V—Word Relatives

_____

_____

_____

Trace:        *original*

_____

_____

_____

Sentences:        **Original** drawings are valuable.
        I want the **original** of that letter.
        This painting doesn't look **original**.

**ELEVENTH WEEK: Thursday**

Word 54:      un doubt ed ly

Pronunciation:  _____

Image:         unDOUBTedly

_____

_____

_____

Bond:          He was unDOUBTedly without a
               DOUBT.

_____

_____

_____

Trace:         *undoubtedly*

_____

_____

_____

Sentences:     **Undoubtedly**, you are right.
               It was **undoubtedly** the work of a thief.
               It's the real thing—**undoubtedly!**

**ELEVENTH WEEK: Friday**

Word 55:      e di tion

Pronunciation:       _____

Image:       EDITion

_____

_____

_____

Bond:       I will EDIT this EDITion.

_____

_____

_____

Trace:       *edition*

_____

_____

_____

_____

Sentences:       Edition after edition was sold out.
                  This is the edition I want.
                  He owns a first edition.

Review: 10 Sentences on Saturday

_____

_____

_____

_____

_____

_____

_____

_____

_____

_____

## 5 Sentences on Sunday

_____

_____

_____

_____

_____

**TWELFTH WEEK:** Monday

Word 56:  op por tu ni ty

Pronunciation:  _____

Image:  opPORTunity

_____

_____

_____

Bond:  Take the opPORTunity to visit the PORT.

_____

_____

_____

Trace:  *opportunity*

_____

_____

_____

Sentences:  **Opportunity** is supposed to knock once.
This is the **opportunity** I've wanted.
Give them every **opportunity**.

TWELFTH WEEK: Tuesday
Word 57: mur mur

Pronunciation: _____

Image: MUR MUR

_____

_____

_____

Bond: Say MUR twice and you MURMUR.

_____

_____

_____

Trace: *murmur*

_____

_____

_____

Sentences: **Murmur** the word, but don't shout.
A strong **murmur** of approval was heard
in the crowd.
It is more than a **murmur**.

**TWELFTH WEEK:** Wednesday

Word 58:     ac cept a ble

Pronunciation:    _____

Image:     ACCEPTable

      _____

      _____

      _____

Bond:     If it is ACCEPTABLE, you are ABLE
to ACCEPT.
See VI—The "ABLE-IBLE" Ending

      _____

      _____

      _____

Trace:    *acceptable*

      _____

      _____

      _____

Sentences:    **Acceptable** reasons were given.
It is not **acceptable** to all.
Make sure the amount is **acceptable**.

**TWELFTH WEEK: Thursday**

Word 59:      bear ing

Pronunciation: _____

Image:        BEARing

              _____
              _____
              _____

Bond:         He was BEARing a BEAR on his back.

              _____
              _____
              _____

Trace:        *bearing*

              _____
              _____
              _____

Sentences:    **Bearing** to his left, he came upon the
              house.
              This has no **bearing** on the case.
              The car has a burned out **bearing**.

**TWELFTH WEEK:**   Friday
Word 60:            fare well

Pronunciation:      _____

Image:              FAREwell

                    _____

                    _____

                    _____

Bond:               He waved FAREwell after paying his
                    FARE.

                    _____

                    _____

                    _____

Trace:              _farewell_____

                    _____

                    _____

                    _____

Sentences:          Farewell was said in short order.
                    He bade farewell to his men.
                    Let me offer you a fond farewell.

Review: 15 Sentences on Saturday

_____

_____

_____

_____

_____

_____

_____

### 1 Paragraph (next page)
### Sunday Morning

_____

_____

_____

### 1 Paragraph Sunday Evening

_____

_____

_____

_____

**Review Paragraphs:** Third Month

When you have done these paragraphs you have completed your ninety day trial. You ought to feel better about spelling now. A word is no longer your boss. You've changed places. Don't stop here. Get after other words that bother you.

The first paragraph below covers 41-60. The second reviews a selected list from the 1-40 group. Any time you want to check yourself on all sixty, just turn to the "Advanced List" in the Appendix.

**I.**

The second **edition** of the book included an **extraordinary** tale of Beppo, a poor farmer who had been secretly appointed **guardian** of a boy who would some day be **sovereign** of the land. At the time, a **committee** of court officials had been ruling the **monarchy,** and the leader **undoubtedly** had hopes that he could be made so **acceptable** that the **original** prince would never be **duly** crowned. However, despite his shabby **clothes,** the lowly field worker decided to go to the palace. He bade **farewell** to his young charge, and promised that only a **miracle** would destroy the **opportunity** to become king.

Beppo arrived just **prior to** a move that had been planned to seize the throne. Of course, he was not **cordially** greeted, but his fine **courtesy** and dignified **bearing** caused a **murmur** of protest to be raised against his dismissal. The proof that the real prince was alive brought great joy to the people. Thus did a **peasant** save a king.

**II.**

That television has become a **permanent** part of American

life is a definite fact. Despite the criticism that has been raised on occasion, every authority in the field agrees that more benefit than harm will eventually occur. It is true the exhausted viewer has not yet learned to use his judgment in selecting the excellent programs over those that merely interrupt his normal activities. Nevertheless, as the novelty wears off, it will become necessary for the studio executive to ascertain whether quantity can take the place of quality. Certainly greater acquaintance with this form of entertainment will improve public taste. Then, if only for financial reasons, a recommendation for good presentations will be possible. People of good sense will decide that junk doesn't warrant their attention.

**Write Words Incorrectly Spelled Below:**

_____

_____

_____

**Compose Paragraph After Study of Missed Words:**

_____

_____

_____

# IX

# General Program

You've proved to yourself that you too can be a good speller. But please don't get smug about it. There are probably a number of common words that still need study. Moreover, you will occasionally meet new words to master. But from here on you are on your own. All you need is a long-range plan. We will give you a ten step program, but only *you* can put it into action.

1. Get a looseleaf notebook. Divide it into three sections. Reserve the first section for any word you use frequently and misspell almost always. Arrange the words as was done in the "Ninety Day Trial." Give each entry THE TREATMENT.

   Label the middle pages "Rarely Used—Like to Know." These will be words you hear now and then, but are not the bread and butter of your daily language diet. Save them for a time when you can be selective about adding to your stock.

   In the final section list the words you have mastered. Set them up in groups of ten under the heading "Mastered List." When you have accumulated this number, compose a paragraph—a story, description, anything—using the former demons. Occasionally ask someone to dictate what you have written so that you can test yourself. Any time you misspell a word in this section, put it back to the beginning, and start all over again with it. Any error shows that you haven't established the correct habit yet.

2. Take your time. Never handle more than **one word a day**. Remember also that a few minutes at a time spread over three periods of the day are far better than six minutes spent all at once. That's worth repeating: 3 minutes in the morning, 1½ in the afternoon, and 1½ in the evening—SIX MINUTES A DAY ARE ALL YOU NEED TO MASTER ANY WORD.

3. Practice writing words **without stopping in the middle for any reason**. Trust your hand. If you have the right habit, you will spell the word right. If not, put the word in section I of your notebook, and give it THE TREATMENT. That old saying applies perfectly to spelling: "He who hesitates is lost."

4. Write legibly. Don't worry about the beautiful kind of handwriting few of us can imitate. But if you want to write an E, let there be no doubt it is an E. Every letter should be clear. Mechanical accuracy will increase your confidence.

5. After you complete any piece of writing, re-read it with care, even if it is a note dashed off in pencil. So-called typographical errors are errors just the same.

6. Once you master a word, use it often. This will help you practice. And you will prove to yourself that you are no longer afraid of misspelling.

7. If you find crossword puzzles amusing, by all means work them. You probably rarely remember a new word from them, but they do offer good spelling review. Word building games can be helpful, too.

8. When you listen to the radio, or watch television, keep a pad nearby. Write some of the words you hear, especially those you've had trouble spelling before. DO THIS AS YOU LISTEN! If you can write the words correctly while you are concentrating on a program, they are yours for a lifetime.

9. Watch your speech. If someone says a word differently from the way you pronounce it, look it up. Remember the case of Mr. D, the man with the automobile accessories stores? His spoken mistakes came to roost in his writing.

10. Don't quit! You may be full of fight for a few weeks. Then you may get that let-down feeling. Don't give in. You can do this job easily, quickly—if you get stubborn about it.

. . .

Incidentally, learning to spell properly isn't all drudgery. You can have fun with words, too. The next four chapters will talk about some of the interesting facts in the background of modern spelling. They will show you how to trace word histories, will give you a few amusing examples of mistakes careless spellers make, and will introduce a *new spelling game*.

Each chapter is not intended as the final word on the subject it outlines. You should, however, be able to use the material as suggestions for further investigation on your own. You will improve your spelling and enjoy many hours of pleasant reading.

## Tittle Page

A Handefull
of pleasant delites

Containing sundrie new sonets
and delectable histories, in
divers kindes of Meeter.

Newly devised to the newest tunes
that are now in use, to be sung:
everie Sonet orderly pointed
to his proper Tune.

With new additions of certain Songs,
to verie late devised Notes not
Commonly Knowen, not
used heretofore.

By Clement Robinson
and divers others

AT LONDON

Printed by Richard Lhones: dwel-
ling at the signe of the Rose
and Crowne, neare
Holburne Bridge
1584

# X

# Spelling Long Ago

To the left is what an old song sheet published over three hundred and fifty years ago looked like. Can you find the 14 misspellings, according to today's standards? Notice the strange use of capital letters. You may well wonder how the printer kept his job.

In fact, Mr. Lhones was simply spelling as he pleased. But there were no accepted authorities then, and each writer or printer was free to be his own dictionary. For instance, you could even beat Shakespeare in a modern spelling bee. Here is the first page of his greatest play. What 14 words would Miss Kitteridge at Billboard High School mark wrong?

"The Tragicall Historie of

HAMLET

Prince of Denmarke

Enter two Centinels (now called Bernardo & Francisco)

1. Stand: who is that?
2. Tis I.
1. O you come most carefully upon your watch,
2. And if you meete Marcellus and Horatio
   The partners of my watch, bid them make haste.
1. I will: See who goes there.

Hor. Friends to this ground
Mar. And leegemen to the Dane
    O farewell honest souldier, who hath releeved
    you?
1. Bernardo hath my place, give you good night
Mar. Holla, Bernardo
2. Say, is Horatio there?
Hor. A peece of him.
2. Welcome Horatio, welcome good Marcellus.
Mar. What hath this thing appear'd againe tonight.
2. I have seene nothing.
Mar. Horatio sayes tis but our fantasie,
    And wil not let beliefe take hold of him,
    Touching this dreaded sight twice seene by
    us, . . ."

Even the great John Milton, author of "Paradise
Lost," would be given the dunce cap in an eighth grade
English class today. This selection from a poem on his
twenty-third birthday is full of errors in spelling, punctuation, and capitalization—according to the way we
would write.

"How soone hath Time the suttle theefe of Youth
    Stolne on his wing my three & twentith yeere
    my hasting days fly on with full careere
    but my late spring no bud or blossome shew'th

Perhapps my semblance might deceave ye truth
    that I to manhood am arriv'd so neere
    & inward ripenesse doth much lesse appeare
    that some more tymely-happie spirits indu'th"

Before you start saying, "What was good enough
for the masters is good enough for me," you must

realize that it was only because the writers themselves began to try for some sort of regularity that modern spelling emerged. They recognized the eventual confusion that would result from spelling by ear. By the eighteenth century, great progress toward uniformity had been made. In one of the first magazines ever published, "The Spectator," edited by Joseph Addison and Richard Steele, we can see fewer differences from our style of writing than existed during the reign of the first Elizabeth.

"                    Thursday, March 1, 1711
                                        . . . . I
had not been long at the University before I distinguished myself by a most profound Silence. For during the Space of eight Years, excepting in the publick Exercises of the College, I scarce uttered the Quantity of an hundred Words; and indeed do not remember that I ever spoke three Sentences together in my whole Life . . ."

By the time Boswell had stopped recording the life of Dr. Johnson in the latter half of the eighteenth century, a page of a London manuscript would have shown few surprises to us.

Oddly enough, however, we Americans took longer to straighten out our letters and punctuation marks. That is partly why some experts claim that our version of English is actually older in form than the modern British.

Less than two hundred years ago, when England was beginning to standardize its spelling, our forefathers were still spelling by ear. In this selection from a charming story about a trip to New York from Boston, Sarah Kemble Knight would have fitted in nicely with English writers who lived a hundred years before her.

"I was Interogated by . . . the Eldest daughter of
the family, with these . . . . words, (viz.) 'Law
for mee-what in the world brings You here at this
time a night?—I never see a woman on the Rode so
Dreadfull late, in all the days of my versall life.
Who are You? Where are you going? I'me scar'd out
of my witts' . . . . when in comes my Guide-to him
Madam turn'd Roreing out: 'Lawfull heart, John, is
it You?—how de do! Where in the world are you
going with this woman? Who is she?'"

You will agree that loose spelling is interesting, and
certainly colorful. But failure to use agreed-upon spellings eventually would have led in writing to what hap-
pened in nations where dialects became too widespread
and numerous. It is not unusual for some countrymen to
speak the same basic language, but fail to understand
one another because of the difference in dialect. Be glad
that *you* can point to any word and say,

"This is how it should be spelled!"

## · XI ·

# Spelling and the Family Tree

Tracing words to their original sources can be fascinating. There are many interesting stories behind modern usage. But apart from the entertainment you can have learning the history of a particular word family, you can also gain valuable aid in your spelling problems.

For example, in the days of the Romans, when a man was an officeseeker he was required to wear a white toga or robe to let the people know that he was anxious for their votes. CANDIDUS is the Latin term for "robed in white." Hence we have the present use of the word CANDIDATE for one who is trying to be elected.

Knowing this fact can help you establish a bond with the difficult part of the word, in this case the DID syllable. Thus, while a good association is always useful, an enriched understanding of the meaning is so much the better.

Here are some additional derivations that make good reading as well as strong bonds. Get into the habit of checking the family tree of every word you look up. It might sound silly if you told someone you spent a few hours "reading" the dictionary. But in fact it can be as much fun as a novel.

**ABUNDANCE.** This is also from the Latin AB (from) and UNDA (wave). Since water is very plentiful, anything appearing in wave-like quantities would be abundant. Note the A in UNDA as a bond for **Ance.**

**ADJECTIVE.** Here it is AD (toward, at) and JACERE (to throw). These words are literally thrown at others (nouns) to make them clearer or more colorful. The DJ combination stands out this way, doesn't it?

**ALPHABET.** The first two letters in Greek are ALPHA and BETA. The word therefore means nothing more than the "A, B's." Note the PH in ALPHA for your spelling aid.

**BARBAROUS.** The Greeks thought any language other than their own crude, rough, uncivilized. They referred to strange foreign sounds as BAR-BAR, nonsense sounds. Note how the first two syllables of the word are merely repeats, thus helping you remember the two A's.

**BOYCOTT.** Captain Boycott was an agent for an Irish landlord whose rents were very high. The collector was subjected to social isolation as a protest by the people. Somehow we seem to remember the spelling of a name more readily than some words so that perhaps you will not forget to use the double T when you write BOYCOTT.

**CHAUVINISM.** Nicholas Chauvin was a member of Napoleon's army, and he was so intensely patriotic that gradually he became a joke among his associates. Spelling the name right helps you over the major hurdle in the word.

**DAHLIA.** The Swedish botanist, DAHL, had this flower named after him. Don't leave that H out!

**DISASTROUS.** We go back to Latin for DIS (against)

and ASTRA (stars); anything happening contrary to the stars, or good fortune, would be DISASTROUS. Note the TR combination in ASTRA. Don't put any letter between the two when you write the word.

**DUFFEL.** This came from a town in England where a type of rough woollen cloth was made. Today the duffel bag is made of canvas, but the spelling of the town is still with us.

**EXHILARATE.** Again we are in ancient Rome where we meet EX (out of) and HILARIS (cheerful); anything that produces a good feeling **exhilarates**. Note the LAR, and keep the A there.

**EXORBITANT.** This really means "out of the orbit," or unusually above the average. Start with EX, add ORBIT, and there you are.

**INNUENDO.** IN (toward) plus NUERE (to nod) combine to give us a word that applies to a statement that doesn't make its point directly but sort of nods in the right direction. You can see where we get the two N's.

**LISTERINE.** It was easy for this product to take the name of the English scientist, Lord Lister, and make a word out of it.

**LUNATIC.** You can remember the A in this word by recalling that it comes from LUNA (the moon). An old superstition claimed that one who stared at the moon would go mad.

**MACADAM.** The Scottish engineer who thought of a new road-surfacing material lent his name to the product.

**MAUSOLEUM.** In 353 B.C. the wife of King Mausolus ordered a magnificent monument erected in his memory. Start with the name and the rest is easy.

**MESMERIZE.** F. A. Mesmer, an Austrian doctor and hypnotist, found his name attached to the technique of causing people to fall asleep or lose their wills. The name itself isn't hard at all.

**NICOTINE.** Jacques Nicot, the French ambassador at Lisbon, sent some plants back to one of the DeMedicis. Judging from modern advertising, he didn't do us a favor because he's the one (at least in the word) we try to get rid of. Note the OT.

**PANDEMONIUM.** When a home run is hit and pandemonium reigns, the place is really full (pan) of demons (demonium). Put the demon in the middle and you chase his spelling friends away.

**QUARANTINE.** Formerly, when a person had a communicable disease, he was required to stay indoors for 40 (quaranta) days. Today the period is shorter, but the ARA combination has not changed.

**SACRILEGE.** Some shady customers used to like to collect (legere) sacred (sacri) objects. The trouble was that they didn't bother to ask anyone's permission, and now SACRILEGE, with the E from LEG, implies an act or statement against religious beliefs.

**VULCANIZE.** The Norse god VULCAN would forge and hammer weapons for his fellow inhabitants of the clouds. Now he has been reduced to a tire patch.

**WORSTED.** This is just the name of an English town, and the R is a typical silent British letter.

**ZINNIA.** The German botanist, J. G. Zinn, has been immortalized by this lovely flower. Note the double N.

· Of course, these twenty-five are but a handful of the thousands of word histories waiting for you to uncover their mysteries. And more often than not, the illogical modern spelling is the result of the odd names and language combinations that were taken bodily into our collection. This is one more time that you can look to the ancestors for the faults in the descendants.

**If You Want to Read More:**

Highly entertaining style, brief little stories, charming illustrations:

*In A Word*—Margaret S. Ernst, James Thurber. (Knopf)
*Word Histories*—Wendell Herbruck. (Dorset)

Extensive coverage, very scholarly, literally stuffed with language lore:

*Thereby Hangs a Tale*—C. E. Funk. (Harper)
*The American Language*—H. L. Mencken. (Knopf)
*The Loom of Language*—F. Bodmer. (Norton)

# XII

# Spelling Boners

**O**rdinarily, when you've been guilty of a misspelling, there is nothing to laugh about. You are seriously concerned about the word, and you should add it to the list that forms your personal study program. However, now and then you may discover that the error has resulted in a rather amusing sentence, especially when the wrong form suggests another word that changes the meaning entirely.

You ought to enjoy these taken from examination papers, newspaper columns, letters, reports, and similar materials. After you've had a chuckle or two, consider how easily all the mistakes, frequently the result of only carelessness, could have been eliminated simply by a more careful re-reading before release to the reader.

Watch out for these "boners." Check what you write. If you find something to laugh about in your work, have a good time, and then get rid of it before anyone else sees it. Here are some samples. In the second sentence the word is used correctly.

·     ·     ·

Paul was visibly **infected** by her words.
She wasn't the least **affected** by his, however.

·     162     ·

The cab driver was **carousing** all over town looking for a fare.

And a police car was **cruising** around looking for him.

· · ·

He was a **stench** upholder of fair play.

So **staunch** a principle should not be suppressed.

· · ·

The Arabs had nothing but the **dessert** to live on, so they didn't have enough to eat.

What else can one grow on a **desert**?

· · ·

Louis XVI was **gelatined** by the Jacobins.

After he was **guillotined**, of course!

· · ·

His signature was so **eligible** that the bank refused to cash his check.

Besides, his handwriting was **illegible**!

· · ·

She was **tide** up all morning.

And she came out cleaner than any soap, with one hand **tied** behind her back.

· · ·

Many of our colonies were founded by people who had been **executed**.

Afterwards, they were **exiled**.

· · ·

Salt Lake City is a place where the **Morons** settled.

The Mormons weren't too happy about them.

· · ·

Some southern families employed **tooters** for their children.
Could the **tutor** play the tooter?

．　　　　　　．　　　　　　．

Typhoid fever can be prevented by **fascination**.
**Vaccination** is equally helpful.

．　　　　　　．　　　　　　．

They recommended that I read "The Queen's **Neckless**."
I never did find out how she could wear a **necklace**.

．　　　　　　．　　　　　　．

When I buy things, money is no **objection**.
But my **object** is to keep the price down.

．　　　　　　．　　　　　　．

My mother is what most people would call a **warrior**.
Poor papa is the **worrier**.

．　　　　　　．　　　　　　．

He graduated **semi** cum laude.
If he had doubled his marks, he might have made **summa**
cum laude.

．　　　　　　．　　　　　　．

I hope that some **sore** of truce will come in the future.
This **sort** of thing leads to wars.

．　　　　　　．　　　　　　．

George ate a lonely meal in the **dinning** room.
His ear plugs made **dining** possible.

．　　　　　　．　　　　　　．

Mr. Kent's favorite meal was **stake** smothered in **unions**.
On the other hand, the president of the local preferred
**steak** with **onions**.

·          ·          ·

The batter hit a **fowl** that went clear out of the park.
I'll bet he suspected **foul** play.

·          ·          ·

Beginning of a letter: "Dear **Anut** Sally,"
Really, frankness can go just so far, even with an **aunt**!

·          ·          ·

It was just to make sure that no one would **enroach** on his
territory.
Nor did he want to **encroach** on theirs.

·          ·          ·

# XIII

# Spellagrams

You have probably tried your hand at crossword puzzles, anagrams, cryptograms, and other word games. However, most of these are not very helpful for sharpening spelling habits. Either there is too much to do, or sufficient stress is not laid on letter combinations directly.

This new game, the SPELLAGRAM, has been designed to be of value *especially* to those who have spelling problems. Once you have gotten the general idea, you'll find it both instructive and fun. You can make the SPELLAGRAM a fascinating parlor game. We'll tell you how later. And, by the way, there are three forms! When you tire of one, play another. Here are the rules.

## Spellagram — Form A

NECINECOSC                    DROBIFS

_ _ _ _ _ _ _ _ _ _           _ _ _ _ _ _ _
(one's inner self)            (prohibits)

CLASPIE                       GREELIVISP

_ _ _ _ _ _ _                 _ _ _ _ _ _ _ _ _ _
(particular)                  (favors, advantages)

166

**Rules**

1. The four blanks represent words which when worked out will read like a telegram message. Each space in the blank is for one letter.

2. Above the blank is the word that belongs in the spaces, but it is in scrambled form.

3. Below the blank is the definition of the word. This is to give you a hint.

4. Your job is simply to use the meanings to help you unscramble the words so that the message reads correctly. In this case, you would finally arrive at CONSCIENCE FORBIDS SPECIAL PRIVILEGES.

5. Note that *every letter in the scrambled word must be used.* Cross each one out as you place it in its proper space.

6. If you have used all the letters, but in the wrong order, you are charged with a misspelling.

7. The scoring is easy. Count the letters in the word missed, and subtract the sum from the total number of letters in the message. For example, this one has 34 letters in all. If you had missed PRIVILEGES, you would take 10 from 34, leaving you with the final score of 24.

Spellagram — Form B

This is the second form of the game.

8

_ _ _ _ _ _ _ _

(set apart)

8

_ _ _ _ _ _ _ _

(accommodations)

9

_ _ _ _ _ _ _ _ _

(usable, at hand)

11

_ _ _ _ _ _ _ _ _ _ _

(at once, now)

| | | | |
|---|---|---|---|
| A A A A A A A | I I I | Q | U |
| B | L L L | R R R | V |
| D | M M | S S | Y |
| E E E E E E | P | T T T | |

Rules

1. The number above the blank indicates how many letters there are in the word.

2. As in Form A, the definitions below the blanks are hints about the words needed to complete the message.

3. Below the puzzle are listed the letters to be used in filling in the spaces.

4. When you have decided on a word, cross out the letters required to write it, and put the word in the blank.

5. Do this until you have completed the message.

6. Naturally, if you have misspelled any words, you will find a shortage of some letters, or too many of others. Thus you will be forced to check your work. Remember; ALL LETTERS MUST HAVE BEEN CROSSED OUT WHEN YOU HAVE FINISHED.

7. Here, too, you score by deducting the number of letters of each wrong word from the grand total. For example, this message is: SEPARATE QUARTERS AVAILABLE IMMEDIATELY, 36 letters in all. If you misspelled SEPARATE, your score is 36 less 8, or 28.

You can form teams among your friends. Each side makes up the SPELLAGRAMS for the other, or a neutral party does the work for both sides. Here's how you keep score:

1. In any series or round, the SPELLAGRAM for both sides must have the same number of letters.

2. Time the period it takes each team to work out the SPELLAGRAM.

3. Make the usual deductions for errors in spelling as outlined above.

4. Add the difference in time it takes one group to finish as compared to the other.

5. Suppose Team A finishes the puzzle accurately in 3 minutes, and Team B in 5 minutes. In a 36 letter game, the final score would be 38-36 in favor of A. Of course, misspellings would further affect the score.

Spellagram — Form C

1. The basic game takes two players. Each player has a pad of paper and a pencil. Also one of the players should have a watch. The player to go first is chosen by the flip of a coin or the drawing of a card.

2. Player A, the first player, selects a word. He then records the word on one slip of paper (out of sight of his opponent) and on another slip of paper he writes the word in scrambled form.

3. At the word "Go!" player A gives the scrambled word to player B.

4. Player B has two minutes to work out the word. If he manages to get the original word, he gets the full number of points corresponding to the number of letters. If he gets another word but still uses up all the letters of the scrambled word, he gets credit for the number of letters minus 1. If he cannot discover a word that uses all the letters, he tries to make any word or words he can, with as many letters as he can. He then gets credit for the number of letters used. But any misspellings mean a zero score for the round.

5. Player B now composes his word, and gives it in scrambled form to A. However, he must use *the same number of letters* player A used.

6. The player who has the highest score at the end of each round has the advantage of leading off

the next round. If the players are tied, the advantage remains with the same player until his opponent has a higher score.

7. Score is kept on the basis of points, and the player who arrives at 100 or more points first wins the game.

8. The game can also be played by four people, two against two, with partners working on the scrambled words.

Here is the start of a sample game:

1. Player A wins the toss.

2. He now selects SMATTER (7 letters) as his word. He writes SMATTER on one piece of paper and on another he writes RASETMT (a scrambled form of SMATTER).

3. At the word "Go!" A gives B the slip of paper with the scrambled word form, and B now has two minutes to unscramble the word.

4. If, within two minutes, B gets SMATTER he is credited with 7 full points (one for each letter in the original word). If he chooses MATTERS, he gets 6 points. (He has used all the letters but has not guessed the right word!) If he gets MASTER he gets 6 points. (There is still one T left over.) If he can think of only MATE or MAST he gets only 4 points. If he misspells, he gets 0 points.

5. It is now B's turn to give a word to A. B chooses COLLEGE (another 7 letter word) and passes on GLELEOC to A who has two minutes to see what he can do with that patchwork of letters. And so the game progresses. Remember: the next words can be ten letters or eight letters or any number just so that in each round the opponents use words of the same length.

Here are some additional Spellagrams for Forms A and B:

## Additional Spellagrams—Form A

1)
N O V E M T N E R G

_ _ _ _ _ _ _ _ _ _

(rule)

C A N T R E M I N O M O D E

_ _ _ _ _ _ _ _ _ _ _ _ _

(statement favoring)

T U B E L D O Y N D U

_ _ _ _ _ _ _ _ _ _ _

(unquestionably)

P A C L A B E E C T

_ _ _ _ _ _ _ _ _

(welcome)

2)
D E N E N T R U S P E N I T

_ _ _ _ _ _ _ _ _ _ _ _ _

(person in charge)

P L I G E L E N X

_ _ _ _ _ _ _ _

(ejecting)

C O M E S H I S U V I

_ _ _ _ _ _ _ _ _ _

(full of tricks)

T R I M Y O O R D

_ _ _ _ _ _ _ _

(rooms in college)

S P U T A C O N C

_ _ _ _ _ _ _ _ _

(dwellers)

3)

ETOOBULAIM

_ _ _ _ _ _ _ _ _ _

(four-wheeled car)

TIXBIHE

_ _ _ _ _ _ _

(show)

NIGENBING

_ _ _ _ _ _ _ _ _

(starting)

DEWSNEADY

_ _ _ _ _ _ _ _ _

(fourth day)

GOTINCINUN

_ _ _ _ _ _ _ _ _ _

(lasting)

GRASTHIT

_ _ _ _ _ _ _ _

(not bent)

HOGHURT

_ _ _ _ _ _ _

(end to end)

YARRBUEF

_ _ _ _ _ _ _ _

(very cold one)

## Spellagrams—Form B

1)

9                                          11

\_ \_ \_ \_ \_ \_ \_ \_ \_                    \_ \_ \_ \_ \_ \_ \_ \_ \_ \_ \_
(chosen group)                          (assuredly)


7                                          8

\_ \_ \_ \_ \_ \_ \_                          \_ \_ \_ \_ \_ \_ \_ \_
(looks for)                              (full)


10

\_ \_ \_ \_ \_ \_ \_ \_ \_ \_
(being present)


| A A A A | F | N N N N | T T T T T T |
| C C C C C C | I I I | O O | X |
| D D | L | P P | Y Y |
| E E E E E E E | M M | S | |

2)

8                                      5

_ _ _ _ _ _ _ _                    _ _ _ _ _
(trade)                            (time measure)


                10                              7

_ _ _ _ _ _ _ _ _ _              _ _ _ _ _ _ _
(kept running)                   (notwithstanding)


            6                              11

_ _ _ _ _ _                  _ _ _ _ _ _ _ _ _ _ _
(every 365 days)             (holiday observance)


A A A A A E E E E E E M                    R R
B B          H         N N N N N N  S S S S S
C           I I I I I   O O          T T T
D D          L L       P            U U U

3)

7                                                    14

_ _ _ _ _ _ _           _ _ _ _ _ _ _ _ _ _ _ _ _ _
(not native)                      (delegates)


                          9                              8

        _ _ _ _ _ _ _ _ _           _ _ _ _ _ _ _ _
            (warmly)                    (presenting)


                    9                                    9

_ _ _ _ _ _ _ _ _                 _ _ _ _ _ _ _ _ _
        (very good)                     (of money)


                          11

_ _ _ _ _ _ _ _ _ _ _
(working together)


AAAAA           FFFF    NNNNNNN S
CCCC            GG      OOOOOO   TTTT
D               IIIIII  PP       V
EEEEEEEEEE      LLLLL   RRRRRR   X
                                 Y

## ANSWERS

Form A—1) Government recommendation undoubtedly acceptable.

     2) Superintendent expelling mischievous dormitory occupants.

     3) Automobile exhibit beginning Wednesday continuing straight through February.

Form B—1) Committee confidently expects capacity attendance.

     2) Business hours maintained despite annual celebration.

     3) Foreign representative cordially offering excellent financial cooperation.

# Appendix

This section contains 2500 selected words. You will note that they have been divided into three groups—basic (including "100 Spelling Demons"), average, and advanced. This has been done to enable you to find out for yourself just where you fit in terms of general ability.

If you can spell all in the basic list, you are doing about as well as a person with an elementary school background. A score of 100% in the average group indicates that you can hold your own with most people, regardless of their educational training. After you have achieved complete accuracy with the advanced words, you will be able to call yourself a superior speller.

Go through each list systematically. Have someone dictate the trial sentences to you, or look at them rapidly and write them from memory. As soon as you have accumulated twenty words that require further study, take one a day for a month as described in the "Ninety Day Trial." Test the results of your planned attack, and if you make no mistakes, go on to the next group of sentences. In general, then, it is TEST, STUDY, TEST.

One final word. We've said it before. It must be said again. DON'T QUIT! The rewards for your efforts to improve your spelling will be very worthwhile. You will write with confidence. You will avoid frequent embarrassment. Best of all, you will gradually add new words to your vocabulary because you will no longer fear their spelling.

*Basic List*

**100 Spelling Demons**

**Sentences**

### 1-25

1. We can't choose the blue color again.
2. The country doctor is always busy among his people.
3. I believe this business is dear to him because he built it from the beginning.
4. If the cough does make your chest ache, buy something to break it up.
5. There could not have been any answer to why he was coming.

### 26-50

1. Learn grammar early enough and you will find it easy to know what is correct.
2. I heard a hoarse voice and knew that my friend was here.
3. Instead of trying to guess, just try to hear every word.
4. The digging done, he laid the bulbs in loose soil, and watered them for half an hour.
5. Don't lose sight of the fact that they are having forty people to dinner in February.

*Basic List*

## 100 Spelling Demons

### Words

| | |
|---|---|
| ache | done |
| again | don't |
| always | early |
| among | easy |
| answer | enough |
| any | every |
| been | February |
| beginning | forty |
| believe | friend |
| blue | grammar |
| break | guess |
| built | half |
| business | having |
| busy | hear |
| buy | heard |
| can't | here |
| choose | hoarse |
| color | hour |
| coming | instead |
| cough | just |
| could | knew |
| country | know |
| dear | laid |
| doctor | loose |
| does | lose |

*Basic List Continued*

## 100 Spelling Demons

### Sentences

### 51-75

1. It seems that children can tear their new shoes in a minute.
2. There is a separate piece of sugar ready for your tea.
3. Some said the raise was sure to come at once.
4. He often says he meant to read it many times.
5. Making a straight line was much harder since none of them had a ruler.

### 76-100

1. Each week, on Tuesday and Wednesday, the women sell used things.
2. Though very tired, I'm writing tonight.
3. They wrote to ask whether the two boys would come.
4. I am truly too busy to write about the dress which I will wear.
5. There won't be any trouble if it is sent through the store where the whole record is kept.

*Basic List Continued*

**100 Spelling Demons**

**Words**

| | |
|---|---|
| making | they |
| many | though |
| meant | through |
| minute | tired |
| much | tonight |
| none | too |
| often | trouble |
| once | truly |
| piece | Tuesday |
| raise | two |
| read | used |
| ready | very |
| said | wear |
| says | Wednesday |
| seems | week |
| separate | where |
| shoes | whether |
| since | which |
| some | whole |
| straight | women |
| sugar | won't |
| sure | would |
| tear | write |
| their | writing |
| there | wrote |

*Basic List Continued*

### Sentences

#### 101-125

1. Struck by the **automobile**, the **angry animal** ran **across** the **avenue**.
2. The **advertisement** gave the **amount** of salary and the **address** where those **already** eighteen could **apply**.
3. Since the **accident**, the poor boy has been **absent**, and pays **almost** no **attention** to the **alphabet**.
4. **Although** he may not be **around** before late **August** or early **autumn**, we can **appoint** him anyway.
5. At the **army** post last **April**, my **aunt** slipped on a **banana** peel and fell **against** a wall.

#### 126-150

1. The **butcher** sold a **certain** kind of **chicken** at a **cheap** price to **build** up his **trade**.
2. My **brother** took the **chalk** at the **blackboard** and drew a man with a **beautiful beard**.
3. Be **careful** to put the **candle** near the **chair** away from the **bottom** of the **Christmas** tree.
4. The **chief** scout put the **cheese** and a **bottle** of wine on a **board between** the weary travelers.
5. **Change** the **button because** it will rub your **cheek** if you are **careless**.

#### 151-175

1. The **death** of the **conductor** in **December** caused the **company** to **close** the tour.
2. A good **citizen** knows the **danger cities** face when they fail to **collect court** fines.
3. The tired **dentist** poured **cream** into his **coffee**, ate a **cracker**, and then lit a **cigarette**.

## Basic List Continued

4. We must **decide** on a **correct collar** for the **cotton** dress or the **customer** will not buy it.
5. Her **daughter** went to **church** to help her **cousin count** the **copies** of the new prayer books.

### Words

| | | |
|---|---|---|
| absent | beard | church |
| accident | beautiful | cigarette |
| across | because | cities |
| address | between | citizen |
| advertisement | blackboard | close |
| against | board | coffee |
| almost | bottle | collar |
| alphabet | bottom | collect |
| already | brother | company |
| although | build | conductor |
| amount | butcher | copies |
| angry | button | correct |
| animal | candle | cotton |
| apply | careful | count |
| appoint | careless | court |
| April | certain | cousin |
| army | chair | cracker |
| around | chalk | cream |
| attention | change | customer |
| August | cheap | danger |
| aunt | cheek | daughter |
| automobile | cheese | death |
| autumn | chicken | December |
| avenue | chief | decide |
| banana | Christmas | dentist |

## Basic List Continued

### 176-200

1. We expect to pay a dollar and eighty cents for dinner this evening.
2. There are eight different parts to each exercise except the eleventh.
3. Eighteen people came to examine the empty houses and a dozen left a deposit.
4. Two men died some distance from the entrance to the factory when a mound of earth fell on them.
5. Either his education in English during the eighth year had been poor or he had forgotten everything.

### 201-225

1. I am looking forward to using the fourth Friday as a happy holiday.
2. Her husband planted the flower in the garden to avoid a family fight.
3. The hospital announced that the grocery clerk had been hit on the forehead with a heavy object like a hammer.
4. If they are hungry, fifteen grown boys can eat a gallon of ice cream in fourteen seconds.
5. The initials on the handkerchief were a great help in proving the forger had used a foreign name to pass a hundred bad checks.

### 226-250

1. June began to learn to laugh a little in kindergarten.
2. They will marry in January or March, and there is much interest in the match.
3. The length of the language lesson does not matter, so long as you listen.
4. It is known that a loaf of bread from the home kitchen will supply a good measure of iron.
5. Writing a letter in the light of a lazy July day will knock any idea of labor out of your mind.

*Basic List Continued*

| | | |
|---|---|---|
| deposit | family | interest |
| died | fifteen | iron |
| different | fight | January |
| dinner | flower | July |
| distance | forehead | June |
| dollar | foreign | kindergarten |
| dozen | forger | kitchen |
| earth | forward | knock |
| education | fourteen | known |
| eight | fourth | labor |
| eighteen | Friday | language |
| eighth | gallon | laugh |
| eighty | garden | learn |
| either | great | length |
| eleventh | grocery | lesson |
| empty | grown | letter |
| English | hammer | light |
| entrance | handkerchief | listen |
| evening | happy | little |
| everything | heavy | loaf |
| examine | holiday | March |
| except | hospital | marry |
| exercise | hundred | match |
| expect | hungry | matter |
| factory | husband | measure |

*Basic List Continued*

### 251-275

1. Neither my niece nor her mother thought the new mustache suited my nephew.
2. Monday morning the newspaper announced that nineteen men had scaled the mountain.
3. All month he kept the medicine near his bed because he would need it in the middle of the night.
4. Even if he didn't invest another nickel, his money would soon multiply into ninety million dollars.
5. It might be a bad mistake to put a needle or a nail into your mouth.

### 276-300

1. A perfect picture of an orange, peach, and pear won the prize.
2. From October to November, the company ought to offer reduced rates for the ocean trip.
3. People of that period could buy a pencil and paper for a penny.
4. Nothing was heard until two o'clock of the ninth day, when noise in the streets told us peace had come.
5. Wearing his overalls under his overcoat, he brought an ounce or two of milk in a pail to ease the pain of the sick calf.

### 301-325

1. The prime reason for his quest was to receive a promise from the king.
2. Do everything in your power to keep him quiet, and please remember to put a pillow under his head.
3. In a talk lasting a quarter of an hour, the president found time to refer to the low pay of the postman and policeman.

## Basic List Continued

4. It is **possible** the **prescription** slipped from my **pocket** when I took a **quick trip** to the **post office.**
5. In the **restaurant,** the **pretty** girl had some meat with a **plain** boiled **potato,** and then drank half a **quart** of milk.

| | | |
|---|---|---|
| medicine | ninth | pillow |
| middle | noise | plain |
| might | nothing | please |
| million | November | pocket |
| mistake | ocean | policeman |
| Monday | o'clock | possible |
| money | October | postman |
| month | offer | post office |
| morning | orange | potato |
| mother | ought | power |
| mountain | ounce | prescription |
| mouth | overalls | president |
| multiply | overcoat | pretty |
| mustache | pail | prime |
| nail | pain | promise |
| near | paper | quart |
| needle | peace | quarter |
| neither | peach | quest |
| nephew | pear | quick |
| newspaper | pencil | quiet |
| nickel | penny | reason |
| niece | people | receive |
| night | perfect | refer |
| nineteen | period | remember |
| ninety | picture | restaurant |

*Basic List Continued*

### 326-350

1. The sight of silver paper and colored ribbon made sister think of Santa Claus.
2. They sail on the sixth of September and should arrive in seventeen days.
3. Although he called over his shoulder for a sandwich several times, there was no sign of service.
4. The seal hunting season started the seventh, and by the sixteenth some soap and water were very welcome.
5. A desire to sleep cut his eyes like scissors, but he continued to work and smoke because the last sentence had to be written by Saturday.

### 351-375

1. The Sunday school teacher told every student that those who suffer know the true meaning of the soul.
2. Sometimes a tailor will return a summer suit still soiled.
3. The soldier sat down to a supper which started with soup and ended with strong, sweet wine.
4. Every tenant was warned by telephone or telegram that he must sweep his side of the street.
5. When you subtract the price of the tax stamp, those stockings from the south cost something more than ours.

### 376-400

1. This is twice that my uncle has left his theater tickets in his other trousers.
2. They start to travel on the tenth or twelfth and return by the twentieth, a week before Thanksgiving.
3. Together we'll pick twelve men tomorrow, and thirteen more next Thursday.
4. Today the rain drove thirty thousand people toward the exit gates, with not one umbrella among them.
5. Billy tore his pants, but one touch of a thread to his mother's tongue and they were ready for a new trial.

## Basic List Continued

| | | |
|---|---|---|
| ribbon | soldier | tenth |
| sail | something | Thanksgiving |
| sandwich | sometimes | theater |
| Santa Claus | soul | thirteen |
| Saturday | soup | thirty |
| scissors | south | thousand |
| seal | stamp | thread |
| season | still | Thursday |
| sentence | stockings | ticket |
| September | street | today |
| service | strong | together |
| seventeen | student | tomorrow |
| seventh | subtract | tongue |
| several | suffer | tore |
| should | suit | touch |
| shoulder | summer | toward |
| sight | Sunday | travel |
| sign | supper | trial |
| silver | sweep | trousers |
| sister | sweet | twelfth |
| sixteenth | tailor | twelve |
| sixth | teacher | twentieth |
| sleep | telegram | twice |
| smoke | telephone | umbrella |
| soap | tenant | uncle |

*Basic List Continued*

### 401-425

1. The visitor can't understand how the United States is governed until he has seen Washington.
2. Without warning, a wasp stung the wagon driver who had gone for a walk to get some water.
3. By a voice vote, the group approved the idea to watch and wait for the results of the wage conference.
4. The warm weather was not usual, and the vegetable crop in the village would grow that much sooner.
5. While he will let you weigh him, he will not welcome any effort to wake him up to the need of a trim waist.

### 426-450

1. Yesterday that young woman became the wife of the owner of the zinc mine.
2. Your answer was worth zero because you described the wrong zone.
3. The zoo was proud of the white fox, whose arrival last year had created great wonder.
4. On his winter vacation he woke early every day to don his yellow skis and zigzag along the trails with the zeal of a boy.
5. Without a care in the world, he ate his dinner with great zest, and then looked out of his window as the plane began to zoom along at an ever faster rate.

## Basic List Continued

| | |
|---|---|
| understand | white |
| United States | whose |
| until | wife |
| usual | window |
| vegetable | winter |
| village | without |
| visitor | woke |
| voice | woman |
| vote | wonder |
| wage | world |
| wagon | worth |
| waist | wrong |
| wait | year |
| wake | yellow |
| walk | yesterday |
| warm | young |
| warning | your |
| Washington | zeal |
| wasp | zero |
| watch | zest |
| water | zigzag |
| weather | zinc |
| weigh | zone |
| welcome | zoo |
| while | zoom |

## Average List

### Sentences
#### 1-25

1. According to experts, an actor or actress must be born with ability and cannot acquire it.
2. Afterward I shall accompany you to the affair because it will be to your advantage to accept the award.
3. To go abroad sounded like good advice, but her absence would be an admission of the actual reason for leaving.
4. We absolutely cannot acknowledge your pass since the addition of secret work forces us to abolish former rules of admittance.
5. Those who adopt this country should develop an accent that people admire, and can accomplish this by attending schools that advertise courses in speech.

#### 26-50

1. So anxious was he to work in the airplane factory that any apartment near it would appear to be agreeable.
2. Blind ambition refuses allegiance even to the altar, and will answer any appeal that feeds its appetite for power.
3. The amendment to the law forced each agency not to approve an applicant who was an alien.
4. Your approach to the argument would be of amusement to anybody, but does not alter the facts.
5. Tim sprained his ankle in the agriculture course and asked whether anyone would arrange to take his arithmetic homework to his next class.

#### 51-75

1. The arrival of the attorney for the association caused a battle in the assembly.
2. I can assure you that no attempt will be made to assist you with the baggage until every article is checked.
3. With an awful scar on one cheek and a bandage beneath his eye, the beggar looked like a wounded beast.

*Average List Continued*

4. The price for the **barrel** is **beyond** what it was **awhile** ago and has **become** no **bargain**.
5. Many a **backward** glance was cast at the **beefsteak** party on the **beach** as the **balance** of the group left to cast its **ballot**.

## Words

| | | |
|---|---|---|
| ability | agency | arrival |
| abolish | agreeable | article |
| abroad | agriculture | assembly |
| absence | airplane | assist |
| absolutely | alien | association |
| accent | allegiance | assure |
| accept | altar | attempt |
| accompany | alter | attorney |
| accomplish | ambition | awful |
| according | amendment | awhile |
| acknowledge | amusement | backward |
| acquire | ankle | baggage |
| actor | anxious | balance |
| actress | anybody | ballot |
| actual | anyone | bandage |
| addition | apartment | bargain |
| admire | appeal | barrel |
| admission | appear | battle |
| admittance | appetite | beach |
| adopt | applicant | beast |
| advantage | approach | become |
| advertise | approve | beefsteak |
| advice | argument | beggar |
| affair | arithmetic | beneath |
| afterward | arrange | beyond |

## Average List Continued
### 76-100

1. The **boarder** would beat his **breast** and **boast** that every day he read the **Bible** he kept in the hall closet.
2. You may **borrow** the **bicycle**, but don't try a **burst** of speed because the worn **brake** may earn you a **bruise**.
3. According to the **calendar**, the **cafeteria** today will serve corned beef, **cabbage**, and a **biscuit** as light as a cherry **blossom**.
4. With a **breath** of pride, Fenton recalled rising from **bootblack** to **blacksmith** to **candidate** for bureau chief.
5. He decided to **bury** the **bundle** of papers and the **cablegram** under the **bridge** and not **breathe** a word about them.

### 101-125

1. The **children** were ready to **celebrate** when told there was a **choice** between **cereal** and **chocolate**.
2. A **century** later, the letters of the **captain** were found in a small **carriage** left in the **cellar** of the **castle**.
3. He asked the **cashier** for **carfare** to the **capital** where he would get the **certificate** to be a **chauffeur**.
4. A **carpenter** was sent to the upper **chamber** to repair a damp **circle** in the **ceiling** near the **chimney**.
5. Since it was not in his **cheerful** **character** to **cheat** or turn to **charity** for help, he decided to sell his **cattle** instead.

### 126-150

1. To **conquer** the **climate** on the **coast**, **clothe** yourself in **comfortable** fashion.
2. Our **Constitution** states that only **Congress** can **consider** matters that **concern** **commerce**.
3. Good **citizenship** must **consist** of the desire to **complain** about any **condition** against the **common** good.

## Average List Continued

4. After the **concert,** she took her **companion** to a little shop where they could sip a cup of **cocoa** in **complete comfort.**

5. The **complaint** about the new plan of the **college** to **connect** the various schools is that it will **commence** before anyone can **compare** it to the old program.

| | | |
|---|---|---|
| Bible | capital | citizenship |
| bicycle | captain | climate |
| biscuit | carfare | clothe |
| blacksmith | carpenter | coast |
| blossom | carriage | cocoa |
| boarder | cashier | college |
| boast | castle | comfort |
| bootblack | cattle | comfortable |
| borrow | ceiling | commence |
| brake | celebrate | commerce |
| breast | cellar | common |
| breath | century | companion |
| breathe | cereal | compare |
| bridge | certificate | complain |
| bruise | chamber | complaint |
| bundle | character | complete |
| bureau | charity | concern |
| burst | chauffeur | concert |
| bury | cheat | condition |
| cabbage | cheerful | Congress |
| cabinet | children | connect |
| cablegram | chimney | conquer |
| cafeteria | chocolate | consider |
| calendar | choice | consist |
| candidate | circle | Constitution |

*Average List Continued*

### 151-175

1. During the conversation, he offered good counsel about the contract, but failed to convince us to continue with the work.
2. The cottage in the country will contain a long work counter with copper trim.
3. A coward considers his lack of courage in dangerous situations a cruel curse.
4. In the course of repairing the damage to the dairy plant, the crew found a cradle used in colonial days.
5. The daily market curve showed that the custom curtain business was not worth a crumb.

### 176-200

1. Unless you can declare war on the delight offered by dessert, you need not describe how you are going on a diet.
2. His decision to make a declaration that the deal had driven him into debt would deceive no one.
3. The delegate claimed that defeat faced democracy if we allowed economy to destroy our defense plans.
4. After the train had left the depot, the old democrat looked over the deed he had to deliver when he reached his destination.
5. I must differ with the dictionary because this diamond is a descendant of those used to decorate the royal crown.

### 201-225

1. As the duke paused on his way downstairs, he was at ease and looked like an eagle standing at the edge of a cliff.
2. If she did discover that the domestic was dishonest, she would have to discuss it with the district officer.
3. It was difficult to discharge the director because he was so earnest and eager to please.

*Average List Continued*

4. No **doubt** few would **disagree** that we had to **educate** every **druggist** in the new treatment of the **disease**.
5. In **due** time he began to **dream**, and it seemed that his **direct double** was coming in his **direction**.

| | | |
|---|---|---|
| contain | deal | difficult |
| continue | debt | direct |
| contract | deceive | direction |
| conversation | decision | director |
| convince | declaration | disagree |
| copper | declare | discharge |
| cottage | decorate | discover |
| counsel | deed | discuss |
| counter | defeat | disease |
| country | defense | dishonest |
| courage | delegate | district |
| course | delight | domestic |
| coward | deliver | double |
| cradle | democracy | doubt |
| crew | democrat | downstairs |
| cruel | depot | dream |
| crumb | descendant | druggist |
| curse | describe | due |
| curtain | dessert | duke |
| curve | destination | eager |
| custom | destroy | eagle |
| daily | diamond | earnest |
| dairy | dictionary | ease |
| damage | diet | edge |
| dangerous | differ | educate |

*Average List Continued*

### 226-250

1. To avoid an error, enclose the employment slip in an envelope, and mail it to your employer.
2. The engineer seemed to enjoy his effort to make the elevator work by hand as well as by electricity.
3. Everybody was told to be especially careful to make an exact drawing of the engine, and to try not to use an eraser.
4. Before you entertain, try to engage someone to embroider the tablecloth to establish the effect of handmade linen.
5. After the election, he decided to escape to Europe to inspect the new electric plants of the British Empire.

### 251-275

1. In our experience, this is just an excuse to exchange the faucet at our expense.
2. It was an extreme example of a female hat, with a long feather and what seemed like a feast of fruits.
3. The failure of his appeal to the federal courts meant that the state would execute the famous prisoner without further examination.
4. Why doesn't the examiner explain to that fellow that he should become familiar with the export laws?
5. A fault of those who cannot fasten themselves to some faith is that they can give no external expression to their emotions.

### 276-300

1. The foreman of the freight department found it hard to resist frequent dishes of fried fish.
2. Unless you wear a flannel shirt, you will freeze during the flight because it may be your bad fortune to run into some fierce winds.

*Average List Continued*

3. On the following day the funeral was held for the lonely figure who had frozen to death near the fountain.
4. Finally the old florist came forth and asked the feminine customer to forgive him for being late.
5. A country built on a firm foundation of freedom tries to be friendly, but does not frighten easily if rejected.

| | | |
|---|---|---|
| effect | examination | feminine |
| effort | examiner | fierce |
| election | example | figure |
| electric | exchange | finally |
| electricity | excuse | firm |
| elevator | execute | flannel |
| embroider | expense | flight |
| empire | experience | florist |
| employer | explain | following |
| employment | export | foreman |
| enclose | expression | forgive |
| engage | external | forth |
| engine | extreme | fortune |
| engineer | failure | found |
| enjoy | faith | foundation |
| entertain | familiar | fountain |
| envelope | famous | freedom |
| eraser | fasten | freeze |
| error | faucet | freight |
| escape | fault | frequent |
| especially | feast | fried |
| establish | feather | friendly |
| Europe | federal | frighten |
| everybody | fellow | frozen |
| exact | female | funeral |

*Average List Continued*

### 301-325

1. The **garment** found in the **garage** was covered with **generous** smears of **grease** and smelled of **gasoline**.
2. To **furnish** the art **gallery** with **genuine** old **furniture** is one of the first jobs the **governor** will assume.
3. With a **gentle** smile, the lady in the blue **gown** goes toward the door to **greet** the tall **gentleman**.
4. It was **funny** to see the **goose** looking at a **geography** book like a **general** making **future** plans over a map.
5. In great **fury**, Peters rushed out to see who had thrown **garbage** into the **furnace**, but the culprit was **gone** and **further** search was useless.

### 326-350

1. In the **hygiene** class we were told that **hominy** grits with **honey** could not keep one **healthy**, **however** much was eaten.
2. As he took the **harness** off the **handsome** horse, his **hearty** **hello** showed his **happiness** that the **harvest** was over.
3. The **guard** asked for the **honor** to **guide** the **guest** to the **history** classes.
4. So great were her **honest** **grief** and **guilt** that she seemed to be **heading** for a state that would affect her **health**.
5. From the **height** of his window he threw the pot **handle** in a **hurry**, hoping to convince the dog not to **howl** at the **heaven** above.

### 351-375

1. No **immigrant** need remain **ignorant** if he is **industrious** in his efforts to **inquire** and get **information** about his new land.
2. **Industry** and labor will hold an **important** meeting **immediately** and will **include** talk about an **increase**.
3. To show his **independence**, the **industrial** leader refused to **imitate** the **idea** because it would **injure** his name.

## *Average List Continued*

4. We must stress the **importance** of confining certain **insane** types because **improvement** for them is **impossible** and they may cause **injury** to someone.
5. In its **innocence,** youth is **impatient** to be **independent,** and needs the **influence** of older heads to **illustrate** how harmful this can be.

| | | |
|---|---|---|
| funny | grief | idea |
| furnace | guard | ignorant |
| furnish | guest | illustrate |
| furniture | guide | imitate |
| further | guilt | immediately |
| fury | handle | immigrant |
| future | handsome | impatient |
| gallery | happiness | importance |
| garage | harness | important |
| garbage | harvest | impossible |
| garment | heading | improvement |
| gasoline | health | include |
| general | healthy | increase |
| generous | heaven | independence |
| gentle | height | independent |
| gentleman | hello | industrial |
| genuine | history | industrious |
| geography | hominy | industry |
| goes | honest | influence |
| gone | honey | information |
| goose | honor | injure |
| governor | however | injury |
| gown | howl | innocence |
| grease | hurry | inquire |
| greet | hygiene | insane |

*Average List Continued*
### 376-400
1. An invitation was sent to the agent to collect the second installment on the insurance for the crown jewel of the kingdom.
2. By ordering the inspector to investigate the quality of the canned juice, the judge showed a fine sense of justice.
3. Let me introduce Mr. Kent, whose intention during the interview is to interpret the judicial report.
4. After putting some kerosene into a kettle, the janitor, following the instruction sheet, poured it on the insect nest.
5. Our journey to the internal region is to settle the issue, and remove the jealousy that has blown tempers as high as a kite.

### 401-425
1. To gain more knowledge for her license test as librarian, Sally attended every lecture at the library.
2. Label Tom a liar, if you will, but he said only some cheese on lettuce leaves and glasses of lemonade were served at the lawn party.
3. The lawyer told the leader of the legion that new legislation made him liable for the actions of his group.
4. Under the lantern was a sign on the laundry door knob, and I saw I was at liberty to sign a lease for the building.
5. Besides scratching her knuckle, the kitten had put such a knot in the wool on the leather chair that no one could knit with it now.

### 426-450
1. A manual of material needed to manufacture the new locomotive was issued with the machinery.
2. The slight maiden taking her marriage vows with her masculine partner made a lovely picture before the magistrate.
3. Madam, this luxury mattress is sewed by special machine, and is advertised in every leading magazine.

*Average List Continued*

4. It was manifest that the lieutenant could not manage his liquor since he acted as if he had been struck by lightning.

5. People with good manners would not loiter long at the marble staircase, for it was the location of the liquid refreshments.

| | | |
|---|---|---|
| insect | kitten | lieutenant |
| inspector | knit | lightning |
| installment | knob | liquid |
| instruction | knot | liquor |
| insurance | knowledge | location |
| intention | knuckle | locomotive |
| internal | label | loiter |
| interpret | lantern | lovely |
| interview | laundry | luxury |
| introduce | lawn | machine |
| investigate | lawyer | machinery |
| invitation | leader | madam |
| issue | lease | magazine |
| janitor | leather | magistrate |
| jealousy | lecture | maiden |
| jewel | legion | manage |
| journey | legislation | manifest |
| judge | lemonade | manners |
| judicial | lettuce | manual |
| juice | liable | manufacture |
| justice | liar | marble |
| kerosene | liberty | marriage |
| kettle | librarian | masculine |
| kingdom | library | material |
| kite | license | mattress |

*Average List Continued*

### 451-475

1. In his message to the group, the minister had to mention the mortgage on the modest church property.
2. The mistress of the millinery shop had made a model in the modern mode.
3. Minus the mosquito bites, the midnight walk in the meadow would have left a wonderful memory.
4. With a mighty swing of his arm, the miller struck the mechanic, and soon every merchant on the street was watching the mortal combat.
5. A messenger was sent by the military governor of Mexico to ask for supplies of molasses and mineral spirits.

### 476-500

1. It seems to be in the nature of the Negro to have a natural sense of musical movement.
2. People of every nationality pass through the narrow entrance to New York harbor to escape the neglect of their native lands and seek naturalization here.
3. Her neighbor removed the napkin from the mutton stew and, seeing that mold had set in, said nobody should eat it.
4. The naughty boy was mute when the neuter gender was mentioned, and the teacher grabbed him by the necktie with murder in her eye.
5. Knowing the nomination would not come from a neutral source, if he came late, Collins strained nearly every muscle to start the motor.

### 501-525

1. Please notify the oculist that I shall obey his request to come to his office as soon as I get official leave.
2. The odor of cooked oatmeal and an onion being fried in olive oil assailed his nostril.

*Average List Continued*

3. There was **objection** to the **occupation** of the **northern** lands, and he dared not **offend** public **opinion**.
4. The **nurse** took an **oath** before a **notary** that it would be her **obligation** to meet all rules with **obedience**.
5. It did not **occur** to him that it would be a **nuisance** to **occupy** the center of the boat until he had to **oblige** by taking an **oar**.

| | | |
|---|---|---|
| meadow | mosquito | northern |
| mechanic | motor | nostril |
| memory | movement | notary |
| mention | murder | notify |
| merchant | muscle | nuisance |
| message | musical | nurse |
| messenger | mute | oar |
| Mexico | mutton | oath |
| midnight | napkin | oatmeal |
| mighty | narrow | obedience |
| military | nationality | obey |
| miller | native | objection |
| millinery | natural | obligation |
| mineral | naturalization | oblige |
| minister | nature | occupation |
| minus | naughty | occupy |
| mistress | nearly | occur |
| mode | necktie | oculist |
| model | neglect | odor |
| modern | Negro | offend |
| modest | neighbor | office |
| molasses | neuter | official |
| mold | neutral | olive |
| mortal | nobody | onion |
| mortgage | nomination | opinion |

*Average List Continued*

**526-550**

1. One **patron** in **particular** was ready to **oppose** the new **orchestra** unless it included an **organ**.
2. The city **ordinance** stated that the **penalty** for a **peddler** who bothered a **patient** would be the **payment** of a fine.
3. When he felt the **package** slipping out of his **palm**, he turned **pale** because neither **parent** would **pardon** him if he broke the vase.
4. He thought it **peculiar** that the **passport** of the **passenger** **opposite** him in the **parlor** car was being checked.
5. Unless your **partner** has booked **passage** on a fast boat, it will be an **otherwise** **ordinary** task to **overtake** him.

**551-575**

1. A **pleasant** moment at the **picnic** was the playing of a **popular** **piano** piece on the **phonograph**.
2. The **police** asked the **physician** to test the amount of **poison** put into the **pepper** eaten by the **porter**.
3. After the **poll**, every **plumber** in the union gave a **pledge** of ten **per cent** of his wages for the **political** drive.
4. It was a **pleasure** to sit on the **porch** with a **pitcher** of lemonade before us, and have a **polite** talk on **politics**.
5. Temple refused to **perform** at his own **peril** unless a **photograph** were taken of a **portion** of the **plaster** wall that looked ready to fall out.

**576-600**

1. The **priest** was unable to **prevail** upon the **prince** to allow a **prayer** to be said for the **prisoner**.
2. It is **probable** that the department will **proclaim** new **postal** rates to **preserve** the **present** services.
3. If you **prefer** to **prepare** the mixture by the old **process**, **pour** some **powder** into a cup and then add water.

*Average List Continued*

4. Send **postage**, and we will solve your **problem** of how to **practice** the dance **position** in **private**.
5. He had to **pretend** to be able to **produce** any results because he was eager to **procure** the **praise** of the **powerful** men.

| | | |
|---|---|---|
| oppose | pepper | position |
| opposite | per cent | postage |
| orchestra | perform | postal |
| ordinance | peril | pour |
| ordinary | phonograph | powder |
| organ | photograph | powerful |
| otherwise | physician | practice |
| overtake | piano | praise |
| package | picnic | prayer |
| pale | pitcher | prefer |
| palm | plaster | prepare |
| pardon | pleasant | present |
| parent | pleasure | preserve |
| parlor | pledge | pretend |
| particular | plumber | prevail |
| partner | poison | priest |
| passage | police | prince |
| passenger | polite | prisoner |
| passport | political | private |
| patient | politics | probable |
| patron | poll | problem |
| payment | popular | process |
| peculiar | porch | proclaim |
| peddler | porter | procure |
| penalty | portion | produce |

## Average List Continued

### 601-625

1. I propose that we serve prune pudding and pumpkin pie at the end of the program.
2. The professor agreed to promote the pupil when he would prove he could pronounce each word.
3. Every property deed had a purple stamp which the owner had to purchase as proof that a proper deal had been made.
4. To protect the public, the city will prohibit the sale of the product for a profit, and will punish offenders.
5. The purpose the legal profession had in wanting to publish the report was to provide a prompt answer to its critics.

### 626-650

1. With her quantity of raven hair, the queen was easy to recognize as she entered the railroad coach.
2. His refusal to quarrel about the rake showed that he was trying to redeem himself and forget his former record as a rebel.
3. On a recent radio program, a rabbi was asked to recite some prayers that had been found in an old reader.
4. She found a piece of rabbit fur of good quality in her purse, and thought it queer that she couldn't recall whose it was.
5. During the recess, Joe was really quite happy when he was offered some of the raisin cake that was lying on the kitchen range.

### 651-675

1. The reporter asked Father Crowley to relate how he had brought religion to that remote region.
2. A special drive was on to request every regular Republican voter who was a resident to register for the election.
3. It was a relief to learn that Summers, who was held in high regard, would be able to represent the republic even under the new regulation.

*Average List Continued*

4. In moments of **repose**, people can **repent** their sins, **repair** their souls, **regain** their confidence, and **renew** their hope.
5. You must **resist** any desire to **repeat** your **reference** to the incident at the **resort**, even to a **relative**.

| | | |
|---|---|---|
| product | purse | reference |
| profession | quality | regain |
| professor | quantity | regard |
| profit | quarrel | region |
| program | queen | register |
| prohibit | queer | regular |
| promote | quite | regulation |
| prompt | rabbi | relate |
| pronounce | rabbit | relative |
| proof | radio | relief |
| proper | railroad | religion |
| property | raisin | remote |
| propose | rake | renew |
| protect | range | repair |
| prove | raven | repeat |
| provide | reader | repent |
| prune | really | reporter |
| publish | rebel | repose |
| pudding | recall | represent |
| pumpkin | recent | republic |
| punish | recess | republican |
| pupil | recite | request |
| purchase | recognize | resident |
| purple | record | resist |
| purpose | redeem | resort |

*Average List Continued*

### 676-700

1. When the **retail** trade took a **rude** drop, the **salesman** knew it would be hard to **restore** his old **salary**.
2. A platter of **roast** beef, a green **salad**, and a piece of **rye** bread caused the **sailor** to **salute** his host.
3. Hit by a **rough** blow with the **rubber** hose, the **robber** let out a **roar** and fell into the **rubbish** heap.
4. Before I **resume** my talk, I **respectfully** ask my **rival** to **reveal** why his firm sold **rotten** fruit to the hospitals.
5. **Review** the **sacrifice** it took to check the **revolt**, and you can see why this man must **retain** your **respect**.

### 701-725

1. In his **search** to **secure** a good **secretary**, he will **select** only one who is **serious** about her work.
2. The **servant** brought some **sausage** and eggs to the **senator**, and a **shallow** **saucer** of milk for his pet cat.
3. A **scream** had been heard at the **scene**, but evidence was **scarce** since everyone had been able to **scatter** before the police could **seize** a witness.
4. Since we want the **screen** over the **sewer** openings now, don't **scratch** your head like a **scholar** but get your **share** of the work done.
5. You may have to **settle** some **severe** differences of opinion before your **selection** for the post will **satisfy** the **senate**.

### 726-750

1. Even the **shawl** gave little **shelter**, and when a **slight** **shiver** was followed by a **sneeze** she went inside.
2. It is **simple** to **sharpen** the tool so that a **single** turn will cut a **smooth** **slice**.
3. **Somebody** must have given a **signal** to the **sheriff** who has just **shown** his **shield** and taken charge.

*Average List Continued*

4. The society members were sincere when they said that his signature on the letter of resignation was a source of sorrow to them.
5. Kicking off a slipper, she watched the soda clerk in sober silence as he tried to shovel some ice cream into a plate.

| | | |
|---|---|---|
| respect | satisfy | sharpen |
| respectfully | saucer | shawl |
| restore | sausage | shelter |
| resume | scarce | sheriff |
| retail | scatter | shield |
| retain | scene | shiver |
| reveal | scholar | shovel |
| review | scratch | shown |
| revolt | scream | signal |
| rival | screen | signature |
| roar | search | silence |
| roast | secretary | simple |
| robber | secure | sincere |
| rotten | seize | single |
| rough | select | slice |
| rubber | selection | slight |
| rubbish | senate | slipper |
| rude | senator | smooth |
| rye | serious | sneeze |
| sacrifice | servant | sober |
| sailor | settle | society |
| salad | severe | soda |
| salary | sewer | somebody |
| salesman | shallow | sorrow |
| salute | share | source |

*Average List Continued*

### 751-775

1. As the old **statesman** rose on the **stage** to give his **speech**, we sang "The Star-Spangled Banner" with great **spirit**.
2. The retired **station** agent would sit in the town **square** and **spread** crumbs of **stale** bread for his **sparrow** friends.
3. At the **steam** table, I found the choice to be **steak**, **spinach** and corn, or **spare** ribs in a **special** sauce.
4. When the **speaker** made a **statement** about those who **sponge** on the state and **steal** public funds, some **spice** came into his talk.
5. A **splendid** appeal by the chairman broke the **steady** effort of the **standard** bearers of the **southern** group to form a **splinter** party.

### 776-800

1. All of a **sudden**, a shell ripped through a **steel** plate in the **stern** near the **steerage** and caused a **stir** in the engine room.
2. **Strife** had broken out above the **stream** where only **superior** land **strength** would **succeed** in turning back the enemy.
3. He tried to **stretch** his arm, but the **strange** pain in his **stomach** made it a **struggle** to **steer**.
4. By a **stroke** of luck, the **substitute** for the regular **stenographer** was such a **success** that Miss Webb had no need to **summon** help.
5. A **stripe** is in **style** this year, but we **suggest** that you **submit** a few more sketches on the **subject**.

*Average List Continued*

| | |
|---|---|
| southern | steel |
| spangle | steer |
| spare | steerage |
| sparrow | stenographer |
| speaker | stern |
| special | stir |
| speech | stomach |
| spice | strange |
| spinach | stream |
| spirit | strength |
| splendid | stretch |
| splinter | strife |
| sponge | stripe |
| spread | stroke |
| square | struggle |
| stage | style |
| stale | subject |
| standard | submit |
| statement | substitute |
| statesman | succeed |
| station | success |
| steady | sudden |
| steak | suggest |
| steal | summon |
| steam | superior |

*Average List Continued*

#### 801-825

1. To see the actor swallow the sword was a surprise to the surgeon who was once heard to swear it was impossible to do.
2. The supply company had a terrible trip through the swamp since one swarm of insects after another rose from its surface.
3. On a tablet in the old temple, someone with talent had outlined the system of worship under the supreme ruler.
4. If you want the support of the chief teller, don't lose your temper if he refuses to telegraph the money to the sweater concern.
5. I suppose it wasn't odd in the summer to see a man sitting in front of a tenement, suspenders down, shirt tail out, and sweat pouring from his brow.

#### 826-850

1. The tiger has been a thorn in the sides of the people of that territory, and has struck terror in the hearts of the timid.
2. A distant clap of thunder seemed to threaten rain, which we thought would relieve the thirst of the crops throughout the area.
3. Shot in the thigh, the thief tried to escape by the toilet window, but met with total defeat when he slipped on a thimble and fell.
4. A little tomato juice, a piece of toast, and a pipeful of tobacco were enough of a tonic to tide him over until supper.
5. Pointing with his thumb toward the tidy little house, he spoke of a token deposit before title, and therefore asked for a check.

*Average List Continued*

| | |
|---|---|
| supply | territory |
| support | terror |
| suppose | therefore |
| supreme | thief |
| surface | thigh |
| surgeon | thimble |
| surprise | thirst |
| suspenders | thorn |
| swallow | thought |
| swamp | threaten |
| swarm | throughout |
| swear | thumb |
| sweat | thunder |
| sweater | tide |
| sword | tidy |
| system | tiger |
| tablet | timid |
| tail | title |
| talent | toast |
| telegraph | tobacco |
| teller | toilet |
| temper | token |
| temple | tomato |
| tenement | tonic |
| terrible | total |

*Average List Continued*

### 851-875

1. A trailer truck had hit a trolley, and police were unable to clear up traffic in the tunnel for an hour.
2. The tribe had sent the trustee a copy of an original native tune as a tribute to his good treatment of them.
3. If you twist some plastic twine around that ugly tube, you can use it as a towel bar.
4. Since no trace of the typist could be found, the treasurer went to the typewriter and pounded out the transfer of funds report.
5. On his return from a tough treasure hunt, the traveler ate the turkey gladly, but refused the cooked turnip.

### 876-900

1. Not knowing it was unlawful to unbutton his uniform, the unfortunate cadet was caught and sent upstairs.
2. Although a bit unusual, the university will undertake to unite the union members by offering a course in labor problems.
3. The urge to be useful is a universal trait, and people are unhappy if old age or illness makes them feel useless.
4. For some unknown reason, a boy climbed upward to an unfurnished room in the upper story, and was unseen by us.
5. Unlike his unhealthy brother, Jim will find the uneven, untried climate harmless, unless we are mistaken.

*Average List Continued*

| | |
|---|---|
| tough | unbutton |
| towel | undertake |
| trace | uneven |
| traffic | unfortunate |
| trailer | unfurnished |
| transfer | unhappy |
| traveler | unhealthy |
| treasure | uniform |
| treasurer | union |
| treatment | unite |
| tribe | universal |
| tribute | university |
| trolley | unknown |
| trustee | unlawful |
| tube | unless |
| tune | unlike |
| tunnel | unseen |
| turkey | untried |
| turnip | unusual |
| twine | upper |
| twist | upstairs |
| typewriter | upward |
| typist | urge |
| ugly | useful |
| unable | useless |

*Average List Continued*

#### 901-925

1. The usher tried in vain to reach the vacant seat, but to his utter disgust the small man was the victor in the race.
2. Veto that bill and you will vex everyone in the valley who will consider it a victory for the forces of vice.
3. On her vacation she loved to walk in the vale where a variety of valuable orchids were everywhere in view.
4. Various meats, including veal, were cooking in the utensil, whose great value was its vapor seal.
5. Every vein of the captain of the vessel stood out as he tried his utmost to verify the report that he had been the victim of a plot.

#### 926-950

1. So weak had the voyage made the weary girl that all she could do was wail and weep.
2. He showed a visible wealth of talent with the violin, and it would be a waste not to make playing it his vocation.
3. The waiter had put such a volume of vinegar in the dish that the vile taste made the diner vomit.
4. At the wedding of the wealthy broker, a watchman was hired to keep the grounds void of intruders who might wander in.
5. With a look of virtue on his face, the warden announced with vigor that he had found the weapon in a violet bed.

## *Average List Continued*

| | |
|---|---|
| usher | vigor |
| utensil | vile |
| utmost | vinegar |
| utter | violet |
| vacant | violin |
| vacation | virtue |
| vain | visible |
| vale | vocation |
| valley | void |
| valuable | volume |
| value | vomit |
| vapor | voyage |
| variety | wail |
| various | waiter |
| veal | wander |
| vein | warden |
| verify | waste |
| vessel | watchman |
| veto | weak |
| vex | wealth |
| vice | wealthy |
| victim | weapon |
| victor | weary |
| victory | wedding |
| view | weep |

*Average List Continued*

### 951-975

1. We heard the witness whisper to the widow that he would withdraw from the case if she were willing.
2. Wheat was sent by the western world wherever and whenever it could serve the welfare of the poor.
3. Whatever the wholesale price of the wheelbarrow is, be sure to get the proper width and a rubber wheel.
4. Whence the wine barrel had come was beyond his wisdom, but the weight of it made him pause to wipe his brow.
5. The whistle of the boy coming down from the willow tree stopped short when the wicked old farmer struck him with a wire whip.

### 976-1000

1. The youth became a worker for the Zion movement because he wanted worse than ever to end the woe his people had suffered.
2. He did no more than wrench his wrist, but his main worry was how to worm his way out of this wreck.
3. His career reached the zenith when his wonderful carving of a wooden zebra was judged worthy of the grand prize.
4. I wouldn't mind if yonder wretch would only yawn when I play the zither, but the worst of it is he snores, too.
5. Trying to take the yeast stain out of her woolen wrap, all she did was wound herself on the zipper.

*Average List Continued*

| | |
|---|---|
| weight | woe |
| welfare | wonderful |
| western | wooden |
| whatever | woolen |
| wheat | worker |
| wheel | worm |
| wheelbarrow | worry |
| whence | worse |
| whenever | worst |
| wherever | worthy |
| whip | wound |
| whisper | wrap |
| whistle | wreck |
| wholesale | wrench |
| wicked | wretch |
| widow | wrist |
| width | yawn |
| willing | yeast |
| willow | yonder |
| wine | youth |
| wipe | zebra |
| wire | zenith |
| wisdom | Zion |
| withdraw | zipper |
| witness | zither |

## Ninety Day Trial
### Sentences

#### 1-20

1. A capacity crowd watched the American team win the benefit basketball game.
2. With the cooperation of the salesman, who showed her the catalog, she was able to buy some acceptable clothes.
3. Much criticism was directed against the committee for using its authority without a legal basis.
4. No one in good conscience would issue a bulletin without first trying to ascertain the bearing it would have on the case.
5. Your courtesy in offering to accommodate my acquaintance will be cordially repaid.

#### 21-40

1. A guardian will be duly named to keep definite control over financial matters.
2. By some miracle, the exhausted boys reached the dormitory before their mischief was discovered.
3. In the judgment of the dealer, it would be an excellent edition to add to his collection of classic literature.
4. The chief executive of the government made an extraordinary farewell address.
5. We will not interrupt the building of the extension if we can determine the existence of a proper permit.

#### 41-60

1. Undoubtedly the monarchy would not return since a recommendation had been made to exile the sovereign.

*Advanced List Continued*

2. It will be **necessary** for me to get a **quantity** of slides to meet a **requirement** of the **zoology** class.
3. I heard one **peasant murmur** that the **warrant** for the arrest of the official should contain a **treason** charge.
4. Have the good **sense** on this **occasion** to take a **thorough** grasp of the **opportunity**.
5. Our **original** plan was to sign for a **partial** period **prior** to any **permanent** arrangement.

### Ninety Day Trial
### Words

| | | |
|---|---|---|
| acceptable | definite | monarchy |
| accommodate | determine | murmur |
| acquaintance | dormitory | necessary |
| American | duly | occasion |
| ascertain | edition | opportunity |
| authority | excellent | original |
| basis | executive | partial |
| basketball | exhausted | peasant |
| bearing | existence | permanent |
| benefit | extension | prior |
| bulletin | extraordinary | quantity |
| capacity | farewell | recommendation |
| catalog | financial | requirement |
| clothes | government | sense |
| committee | guardian | sovereign |
| conscience | interrupt | thorough |
| cooperation | judgment | treason |
| cordially | literature | undoubtedly |
| courtesy | miracle | warrant |
| criticism | mischief | zoology |

## Advanced List Continued
### Sentences
### 1-25

1. Accordingly, we will adjourn this case until you bring a signed affidavit from your accountant that the agreement existed.
2. No adjective could describe his agony as he knelt in the aisle to ask the Almighty for an abatement of his sorrow.
3. An abundance of alcohol always would affect him with an air of abandon and gay adventure.
4. The acknowledgment that use of the alloy would be all right and in accordance with plans was accidentally mislaid.
5. Man will not accustom himself to letting others abridge his freedom, however much they seek to achieve his admiration by speaking affectionately of justice.

### 26-50

1. When the altos joined in the ancient song, our appreciation mounted because the chorus sounded altogether like a group of angels.
2. Apparently, the ambassador had sought the arrangement of an appropriation for his area.
3. From the appearance of things, the operation for appendicitis could not be performed on the arctic explorer because no antiseptic was anywhere to be found.
4. The ambitious architect was glad to announce that his apparatus had been approved for the annual show.
5. Approximately a dozen tutors had tried vainly from every angle to get Roger to appreciate his ancestors, but he remained aloof.

*Advanced List Continued*

## Words

abandon
abatement
abridge
abundance
accidentally
accordance
accordingly
accountant
accustom
achieve
acknowledgment
adjective
adjourn
admiration
adventure
affect
affectionately
affidavit
agony
agreement
aisle
alcohol
alloy
all right
Almighty

aloof
altogether
altos
ambassador
ambitious
ancestors
ancient
angels
angle
announce
annual
antiseptic
anywhere
apparatus
apparently
appearance
appendicitis
appreciate
appreciation
appropriation
approximately
architect
arctic
area
armory

*Advanced List Continued*

### 51-75

1. A large **audience** came to the **balcony** of the **armory** to watch the **banquet** being given for the star **athlete**.
2. On the **average**, he kept ten sacks of **barley available** in his **basement** for the **assistance** of the poor.
3. I shall **assign** an **attendant** to tell the **author** not to **ascend** the platform before the people **assemble** and are seated.
4. You can **assume** it would **astonish** him to learn of the **barbarous** treatment even **babies** were given after the village was **attacked**.
5. Her **beauty** could so **attract** men that they were forever **attaching** themselves, although she kept **assuring** them they would go **bankrupt** buying her presents.

### 76-100

1. On her **blouse** she wore two **cameos** which had **bronze** clips and **butterfly** designs in **brilliant** colors.
2. The **burglar** did not **beware** the dog at the **boundary** of the estate, but one **bestial** growl sent him up the **bough** of a tree.
3. In the **beginning** it was our **belief** that the **bricklayer** had gone over our **budget** by a hair's **breadth**.
4. Who would **boycott** a party where **besides** sandwiches there was a cool **beverage bubbling** in a large **bucket**?
5. At the **burial**, someone **brought** a **bugle** to his lips, as the captain, holding the **bridle** of his horse, stood with head bowed under his **burden** of grief.

## Advanced List Continued

arrangement
ascend
assemble
assign
assistance
assume
assuring
astonish
athlete
attaching
attacked
attendant
attract
audience
author
available
average
babies
balcony
bankrupt
banquet
barbarous
barley
basement
beauty

beginning
belief
besides
bestial
beverage
beware
blouse
bough
boundary
boycott
breadth
bricklayer
bridle
brilliant
bronze
brought
bubbling
bucket
budget
bugle
burden
burglar
burial
butterfly
cameos

*Advanced List Continued*

### 101-125

1. The ceremony was in celebration of the end of the campaign which had carried the champion to the peak of his career.
2. Canoeing down the river, Tom pulled his camera out of its canvas cover so that he could capture the lovely sight of the distant cathedral.
3. When the cargoes arrived at the cannery, the celery and cauliflower crates were unloaded, but the cantaloupe shipment was sent back.
4. As the cavalry swept past the cemetery toward the captive company, the roar of the cannon did not cease.
5. From its office in the capitol, the census bureau announced a new canvass of the changeable population if capable workers could be found.

### 126-150

1. In the chapel, the community choir sang several Christian hymns in commendable fashion.
2. By comparison, the cobbler could claim more chargeable accounts than the clothier.
3. The commission sent a circular through the colony, warning that chauvinism had always been a threat to civilization.
4. According to the report of the chemist, someone with coarse chestnut hair has committed the crime against the colonist.
5. A communication from the circus manager said that under no circumstances would the combination dive be permitted from the top of the column.

*Advanced List Continued*

camera
campaign
cannery
cannon
canoeing
cantaloupe
canvas
canvass
capable
capitol
captive
capture
career
cargoes
cathedral
cauliflower
cavalry
cease
celebration
celery
cemetery
census
ceremony
champion
changeable

chapel
chargeable
chauvinism
chemist
chestnut
choir
Christian
circular
circumstance
circus
civilization
claim
clothier
coarse
cobbler
colonist
colony
column
combination
commendable
commission
committed
communication
community
comparison

*Advanced List Continued*

### 151-175

1. **Confidence** in his **compass** made him **completely** sure he would avoid **confusion** even if he went a **considerable** way into the woods.
2. If neither side will **concede** ground in the matter of **compensation**, you will **compel** me to **conclude** the **conference**.
3. He had to **confess** that he had cheated in the class **competition**, and it was small **consolation** that his **comrade** did not **condemn** him.
4. **Consequently**, after the **compilation** of the facts, everyone could **comprehend** why an effort was made to **conceal** their **connection** with the senator.
5. Although he would try to **construct** a new **composition** for the **complexion** cream, he was **conscious** of the **consequence** of failure.

### 176-200

1. At the **convention**, one doctor told how he had **created** a **continuous** check on the **contagious** disease by setting up a **controlled** group.
2. In a **contemptible** effort to avoid **criminal** charges, the **corrupt** **controller** of the **corporation** left town.
3. Several **countries** on the **continent** organized a **council** in order to **consult** with one another about the proper **conveyance** of defense plans.
4. Only the **continual** sound of a **cricket** disturbed the strange **creature** as he scrawled a bit of **correspondence** with a large **crayon**.
5. **Contrary** to our expectations, the **contractor** had shown a **cordial** interest in our **convenience** by making the porch **convertible** to an all year room.

*Advanced List Continued*

| | |
|---|---|
| compass | consult |
| compel | contagious |
| compensation | contemptible |
| competition | continent |
| compilation | continual |
| completely | continuous |
| complexion | contractor |
| composition | contrary |
| comprehend | controlled |
| comrade | controller |
| conceal | convenience |
| concede | convention |
| conclude | convertible |
| condemn | conveyance |
| conference | cordial |
| confess | corporation |
| confidence | correspondence |
| confusion | corrupt |
| connection | council |
| conscious | countries |
| consequence | crayon |
| consequently | creation |
| considerable | creature |
| consolation | cricket |
| construct | criminal |

*Advanced List Continued*

### 201-225

1. The **delicate** care with which the nurse placed a **cushion** behind the **cripple** seemed to be a **denial** of her reputation for **cruelty.**
2. These **dahlia** seeds will give **delightful** flowers, and if you **cultivate** the **cucumber** patch you will have a **delicious** addition to your summer menu.
3. It was **curious** to see how the **decrease** of supplies in the **cupboard** had made her **dependent** on the **delivery** service.
4. In his **deposition** before the judge, Mr. Cole pointed out the **degree** to which the once **dependable** market had fallen into a **current decline.**
5. A **cursory** glance at the **dense** growth made him decide to **defy** the **decree** of his landscaper not to use the grass **cutter.**

### 226-250

1. From the **description** of the footprints, the **detective** believed that the **difference** in **depth** between the two was **destined** to solve the case.
2. He would **derive** more benefit if he were to **deprive** himself rather than **devour** everything in sight and have **difficulty** later trying to **digest** the food.
3. The **dilemma** he faced was the need to **devote** full time to the **development** of a new **design** for the stamping **device.**
4. In the **directory** was the address of her **despised** relative, but **dignity** would not allow one to **descend** so low as to visit the **disagreeable** man.
5. **Diphtheria** in this **desolate** area would bring **destruction** and **despair** unless **desperate** efforts were made to fight it.

*Advanced List Continued*

cripple
cruelty
cucumber
cultivate
cupboard
curious
current
cursory
cushion
cutter
dahlia
decline
decrease
decree
defy
degree
delicate
delicious
delightful
delivery
denial
dense
dependable
dependent
deposition

deprive
depth
derive
descend
description
design
desolate
despair
desperate
despised
destined
destruction
detective
development
device
devote
devour
difference
difficulty
digest
dignity
dilemma
diphtheria
directory
disagreeable

## Advanced List Continued
### 251-275

1. Her **distress** did not **disturb** those who could **distinguish** real pain and **dismiss** this as a mood that would soon **disappear**.
2. I must say I am **disappointed** at your **discontent**, and I **disapprove** your **distinct** effort to **discourage** the others.
3. To **disobey** would be **disastrous**, but there was no way to **dissolve** the **dispute** without meeting with his **displeasure**.
4. We can **dispose** of the goods on **display**, although it's a **disgrace** to sell such **divine** dresses so low, even at a **discount**.
5. A **discovery** was made in the **dispensary** that certain **distinctive** markings helped remove the **disguise** from the odd skin **disorder**.

### 276-300

1. From his **duffel** bag he took the plan which showed how the **electronic** system would **duplicate** colors without need of **dyeing** the **elegant** cloth.
2. Hardly had the **echoes** of her **doubtful** past faded from the **divorce** trial when the **dreadful** news arrived that she had **drowned** herself.
3. The **educator** called the attention of the **editor** to the **doctrine** that an unstable **economy** will create **division** among the people.
4. When the **draftsman edited** the report of the **electrician**, he suggested an **elementary** way to make the estimate **divisible** into a unit price.
5. Nothing short of an **earthquake** will move **drowsy donkeys**, and it **doesn't** seem strange that sometimes their drivers would be **elated** if one came along.

## *Advanced List Continued*

disappear
disappointed
disapprove
disastrous
discontent
discount
discourage
discovery
disgrace
disguise
dismiss
disobey
disorder
dispensary
display
displeasure
dispose
dispute
dissolve
distinct
distinctive
distinguish
distress
disturb
divine

divisible
division
divorce
doctrine
doesn't
donkeys
doubtful
draftsman
dreadful
drowned
drowsy
duffel
duplicate
dyeing
earthquake
echoes
economy
edited
editor
educator
elated
electrician
electronic
elegant
elementary

*Advanced List Continued*

### 301-325

1. Your rescue of the leader from his encounter with the enormous elephant will entitle you to his eternal thanks.
2. Having lost the esteem of the emperor, Tito would now have to emigrate elsewhere, but he was not equipped for travel.
3. It was not easy for the engraver to estimate the cost of enlarging the emblem because of the erasure in the plan.
4. Billy would embrace the chance to run an errand, especially since mother would soon encourage him to supply entertainment for the guests on the piano.
5. In the emergency, one employee turned his energy upon the equipment in a loyal endeavor to repair it before too much time was lost.

### 326-350

1. Everyone was exhausted by the excess of weeping at the news that Carlos had been exiled and would be expatriated for ten years.
2. One explanation of the failure of the exclusive fashion everywhere was its exorbitant price.
3. Evidence that the trip was over would exhilarate the faithful members of the expedition, and make them cry out in exultation.
4. The exhibit would allow no exception, and if he dared exceed the limits of design he would expose himself to being expelled.
5. To exclaim about a threat of famine would excite the people and cause them to explore why other lands should excel theirs.

## *Advanced List Continued*

| | |
|---|---|
| elephant | everyone |
| elsewhere | everywhere |
| emblem | evidence |
| embrace | exceed |
| emergency | excel |
| emigrate | exception |
| emperor | excess |
| employee | excite |
| encounter | exclaim |
| encourage | exclusive |
| endeavor | exhausted |
| energy | exhibit |
| engraver | exhilarate |
| enlarging | exile |
| enormous | exorbitant |
| entertainment | expatriated |
| entitle | expedition |
| equipment | expelled |
| equipped | explanation |
| erasure | explore |
| errand | expose |
| especially | exultation |
| esteem | faithful |
| estimate | famine |
| eternal | fashion |

*Advanced List Continued*

### 351-375

1. A slight flutter of his feeble hand showed that the forcible feeding was having a favorable effect on what had seemed a fatal illness.
2. Our foremost regret was that we had to forsake this fertile land where fruits of wonderful flavor could flourish all year.
3. A feature of the festival was the showing of a film of the fiery singer who was the favorite actress in the south.
4. It would not be feasible to market the fluid fertilizer unless they were fortunate in getting someone to finance the project.
5. Fidelity is a fixture in marriage and tends to forge happiness for all but the frivolous who flatter themselves on being different.

### 376-400

1. At first the furrier would frown, and then become furious at his futility in learning grammar.
2. The glitter in the gorgeous hair of the gracious actress made her look like a glorious goddess.
3. To fulfill his promise to rid the grounds of every grasshopper, the gardener made gradual use of a fuel oil spray.
4. He was fully prepared to swear it was the gospel truth that he had seen a ghost wearing goggles galloping by on a horse.
5. Every generation in the family seemed to graduate a glazier who was a genius at creating graceful figures in blown glass.

*Advanced List Continued*

| | |
|---|---|
| fatal | frown |
| favorable | fuel |
| favorite | fulfill |
| feasible | fully |
| feature | furious |
| feeble | furrier |
| fertile | futility |
| fertilizer | gallop |
| festival | gardener |
| fidelity | generation |
| fiery | genius |
| film | ghost |
| finance | glazier |
| fixture | glitter |
| flatter | glorious |
| flavor | goddess |
| flourish | goggles |
| fluid | gorgeous |
| flutter | gospel |
| forcible | graceful |
| foremost | gracious |
| forge | gradual |
| forsake | graduate |
| fortunate | grammar |
| frivolous | grasshopper |

*Advanced List Continued*

### 401-425

1. The youthful **heir** was **grateful** for the way his **haughty guardian** was **handling** the affairs of the estate.
2. **Hereafter**, before I buy a tool to check the **growth** of the **hedge**, the **hardware** store will have to **guarantee** it.
3. Paul felt **guilty** about his **hatred** for the **greedy** old man and could **hardly** allow him to lie helpless in the **gutter**.
4. While I may **groan** about it, I **hereby** give you my word that **henceforth** I shall **heartily** welcome the work at the **gymnasium**.
5. Don't **grieve** over the lack of **harmony** but **hasten** to show your **gratitude** that at least the main **grievance** has been removed.

### 426-450

1. **Hurrah** for the **humble hoe** which destroys the **immunity heretofore** enjoyed by the weed.
2. **Herewith** is an example of how this **idol** of the **household** listeners appeals to the **illiterate** who cannot see his **hypocrisy**.
3. In deep, **hollow** tones the organ poured forth the **immortal hymn** of man's **heroic** struggle against the **horrible** forces of evil.
4. Anything blocking the **horizon** is a **hindrance** on a highway and should be removed **immediately** before it produces the **horror** of a crash.
5. Your **ignorance** about animals is beyond **imagination**, but come **hither**, and I shall tell you all about this **immense hippopotamus**.

*Advanced List Continued*

heretofore
herewith
heroic
highway
hindrance
hippopotamus
hither
hoe
hollow
horizon
horrible
horror
household
humble
hurrah
hymn
hypocrisy
idol
ignorance
illiterate
imagination
immediately
immense
immortal
immunity

grateful
gratitude
greedy
grievance
grieve
groan
growth
guarantee
guardian
guilty
gutter
gymnasium
handling
hardly
hardware
harmony
hasten
hatred
haughty
heartily
hedge
heir
henceforth
hereafter
hereby

*Advanced List Continued*

### 451-475

1. The infinite faith every inhabitant had in the imperial ruler's wisdom seemed to indicate that no one could induce them to revolt.
2. If you dare impose an inferior instrument on the artist, you will not only inconvenience him but arouse his indignation.
3. My initial impression of that individual served only to inspire an instant dislike for him.
4. At his inauguration he spoke with intelligence of an indivisible nation, and attacked by innuendo those who would undermine every institution held dear by us.
5. Further inquiry showed that this was one instance where one could inherit a tendency that would incline him toward indigestion.

### 476-500

1. In league with the old knight, Fenton worked out an invention which made invisible all signals sent across the isthmus.
2. The legislature made it a crime for any jeweler to sell without an invoice, and whether he could justify it was deemed irrelevant.
3. In the interior of her handbag was discovered the intimate little ivory figure which the laundress had found irresistible.
4. A poorly labeled bottle of iodine will not kindle much laughter in a laboratory.
5. Irregular jewelry purchases by the jockey forced the board to intercede and turn him over to the jurisdiction of the courts.

*Advanced List Continued*

| | |
|---|---|
| imperial | intercede |
| impose | interior |
| impression | intimate |
| inauguration | invention |
| incline | invisible |
| inconvenience | invoice |
| indicate | iodine |
| indigestion | irregular |
| indignation | irrelevant |
| individual | irresistible |
| indivisible | isthmus |
| induce | ivory |
| inferior | jeweler |
| infinite | jewelry |
| inhabitant | jockey |
| inherit | jurisdiction |
| initial | justify |
| innuendo | kindle |
| inquiry | knight |
| inspire | labeled |
| instance | laboratory |
| instant | laughter |
| institution | laundress |
| instrument | league |
| intelligence | legislature |

*Advanced List Continued*

### 501-525

1. Maybe **mama** wanted a **manicure** because she wished to look like the **majority** when she went for her **literacy** test.
2. The **lonely**, **majestic** figure walked up the **macadam** road toward the **magnificent mausoleum**.
3. Keep this **lively** book on your **mantel** since it is good reading and can **likewise lighten** your **leisure** moments.
4. Her **Majesty** found the **mansion** so **lonesome** that she would **loose** a wail like a caged **lunatic** whenever she was left by herself.
5. In the **meantime** he learned that even a **mature** man would have to be built like a **longshoreman** to **maintain** the **lodge** all year.

### 526-550

1. By her new **method,** the **medium** could with a **mere** wave of her hand **mesmerize** anyone who gave her even **moderate** attention.
2. When the child had the **misfortune** to contract the **measles,** the **midwife** became **miserable** and lost all signs of **mirth**.
3. His **misery** mounted when he saw in the **mirror** that the **mischievous** driver had fixed the **meter** to record extra **mileage**.
4. A **memorandum** regarding the **melon** shipment pointed out that the **merchandise** had a **mixture** of quality and did not meet **minimum** standards.
5. **Meanwhile,** as the sad **melody** was played, he stood **midst** the crowd, wishing to **mingle** with those who had come to the **memorial** services.

## *Advanced List Continued*

| | |
|---|---|
| leisure | meanwhile |
| lighten | measles |
| likewise | medium |
| literacy | melody |
| lively | melon |
| lodge | memorandum |
| lonely | memorial |
| lonesome | merchandise |
| longshoreman | mere |
| loose | mesmerize |
| lunatic | meter |
| macadam | method |
| magnificent | midst |
| maintain | midwife |
| majestic | mileage |
| majesty | mingle |
| majority | minimum |
| mama | mirror |
| manicure | mirth |
| mansion | mischievous |
| mantel | miserable |
| mature | misery |
| mausoleum | misfortune |
| maybe | mixture |
| meantime | moderate |

*Advanced List Continued*

### 551-575

1. By **mutual** consent, the **musician** and his wife decided to move out of the **neighborhood** because the **moist** climate was lowering their **morale**.
2. Although the body of the **monarch** may **molder** beneath his **monument**, the **narrative** of his deeds will live forever in the hearts of the **multitude**.
3. How the **monkeys** had escaped from the **municipal museum** would always remain a **mystery** to the **motor-cycle** officers assigned to catch them.
4. Moreover, his **motive** in wishing to make us **nervous** by talking about a **mysterious monster** was not clear.
5. Nevertheless, the **moral** of the story is that **moisture** in tobacco will no more reduce **nicotine** than sugar will sweeten **mustard**.

### 576-600

1. **Numerous** members of the **organization** came to the **palace** for the **occurrence**, but **pandemonium** broke loose when the king failed to appear.
2. He had **originally** made the **observation** that to **ordain** a minister in an **opera** house was **outrageous**, and most people agreed.
3. **Obedient** though the **orphan** was, he had to offer **opposition** against the effort to **oppress** him for every minor **offense**.
4. It was a **novelty** for us to **observe** how the **oyster** would **occasionally nourish** itself.
5. To **operate** that **orchard** of ours allowed time for only an **occasional** trip to buy some clothing or an **ornament** for the house.

*Advanced List Continued*

| | |
|---|---|
| moist | nourish |
| moisture | novelty |
| molder | numerous |
| monarch | obedient |
| monkeys | observation |
| monster | observe |
| monument | occasional |
| moral | occasionally |
| morale | occurrence |
| moreover | offense |
| motive | opera |
| motorcycle | operate |
| multitude | opposition |
| municipal | oppress |
| museum | orchard |
| musician | ordain |
| mustard | organization |
| mutual | originally |
| mysterious | ornament |
| mystery | orphan |
| narrative | ours |
| neighborhood | outrageous |
| nervous | oyster |
| nevertheless | palace |
| nicotine | pandemonium |

*Advanced List Continued*

### 601-625

1. Papa was **partial** to **peanut** butter in his **pastry**, but in neither of the **pantries** could we find any.
2. People lining the **pavement** could **perceive** the look of the true **patriot** on the faces of the **parachute** troops who were passing in **parade**.
3. Every **paragraph** of the speech he delivered with such **passion** before **parliament** seemed like a **pearl** of wisdom dropped from **paradise**.
4. A good **percentage** of the horses stood **parallel** to each other in the **peaceful pasture**, looking as if they had been retired on **pension**.
5. His **patience** was rewarded when the **patent** office approved his **pattern** for a **penicillin** extractor, and returned it by **parcel** post.

### 626-650

1. The great **persistence** a **pigeon** shows when it travels miles from its **perch** and returns is no **phenomenon** because I have **personally** seen it done.
2. No **phrase** in the **petition** demanded **perfection**, but it sought to **persuade** the governor to grant **permission** for action to be taken.
3. As he leaned against a **pillar** near the **piazza** and breathed the **perfume** of the flowers, a **pistol** shot **pierced** the air.
4. Before the **picnicking** began we thought we would **perish** from **perspiration**, but some **pineapple** juice followed by sandwiches and a **pickle** salad soon revived us.
5. Because his religious **philosophy** was not **permissible** at home, the **pilgrim** became a **pioneer** in search of **perpetual** freedom.

*Advanced List Continued*

pantries

papa

parachute

parade

paradise

paragraph

parallel

parcel post

parliament

partial

passion

pastry

pasture

patent

patience

patriot

pattern

pavement

peaceful

peanut

pearl

penicillin

pension

perceive

percentage

perch

perfection

perfume

perish

permissible

permission

perpetual

persistence

personally

perspiration

persuade

petition

phenomenon

philosophy

phrase

piazza

pickle

picnicking

pierced

pigeon

pilgrim

pillar

pineapple

pioneer

pistol

### 651-675

1. One **premise** of modern **poetry** is that such common things as **potatoes** or **poultry** can become proper subjects for a poem.
2. **Preach** all he might about the value to **posterity** of the **preamble** to the Constitution, the **politician** still offered no **policy** we could understand.
3. She was **practically** mad about the **precious pottery** of the ancient **potentate,** and showed her **preference** by outbidding everybody.
4. A **plunge** from the **platform** was no answer to her **poverty,** even though she had lost every **possession** to a convicted **polygamist.**
5. One should not **precede** the other, but public education and **practical** measures will prevent the **possibility** of a **pneumonia plague.**

### 676-700

1. Since I'm no **prophet,** I shall not **presume** to **prophesy** what **progress** you will make, but what I **prescribe** should help.
2. **Prominent** people considered it a **privilege** to lend their **presence** to the **procession** in honor of the **princess.**
3. **Probably** the old **principle** will be applied, and no one will **preside** over a **primary** election who has not had **previous** training.
4. The **proprietor,** a **prey** to wild schemes before, said there was no **prospect** he would accept this **proposition** without study and **preparation.**
5. Not to **prolong** his talk, the **principal** concluded with the **prophecy** that a large **proportion** of the graduates would **proceed** to college and do well.

*Advanced List Continued*

| | |
|---|---|
| plague | preparation |
| platform | prescribe |
| plunge | presence |
| pneumonia | preside |
| poem | presume |
| poetry | previous |
| policy | prey |
| politician | primary |
| polygamist | princess |
| possession | principal |
| possibility | principle |
| posterity | privilege |
| potatoes | probably |
| potentate | proceed |
| pottery | procession |
| poultry | progress |
| poverty | prolong |
| practical | prominent |
| practically | prophecy |
| preach | prophesy |
| preamble | prophet |
| precede | proportion |
| precious | proposition |
| preference | proprietor |
| premise | prospect |

*Advanced List Continued*

### 701-725

1. There is no **question** that the **publication** will **qualify** for a higher **rating** when it makes **provision** for wider news coverage.
2. Every **reasonable** plan had been tried, and now only **Providence** would bring **prosperity readily** to the **realm**.
3. It was no **puzzle** why the people in the upper **province** did not **protest** over the **quarantine** because they had to **realize** it was for their own good.
4. **Psychology** tells us that **punishment** will not **quench** a strong spirit, but will merely **provoke** it to **pursue** its course all the harder.
5. The **prosperous** farmer enjoyed life, and a **rainbow** or blue sky could **quicken** his **pulse** at the sheer **rapture** of the colors.

### 726-750

1. In his **replies**, the **representative** said he **regretted** that to **relieve** the situation there would have to be a **referendum**.
2. As no **remittance** of a **receipt** was made in my **remembrance**, we'll place the **remainder** of the balance in the accounts **receivable**.
3. To **recede** before public opinion meant to **reject** his ideals, and no man of **renown** could **renounce** his beliefs nor take **refuge** in fear.
4. If you **reflect** on what **remedy** will give you **release**, you will find that **religious** faith may **reconcile** you to your troubles.
5. Let us **rejoice** in the **reign** of this **remarkable** king who allows no **repetition** of the evils we had to **reckon** with before.

*Advanced List Continued*

| | |
|---|---|
| prosperity | recede |
| prosperous | receipt |
| protest | receivable |
| Providence | reckon |
| province | reconcile |
| provision | referendum |
| provoke | reflect |
| psychology | refuge |
| publication | regretted |
| pulse | reign |
| punishment | reject |
| pursue | rejoice |
| puzzle | release |
| qualify | relieve |
| quarantine | religious |
| quench | remainder |
| question | remarkable |
| quicken | remedy |
| rainbow | remembrance |
| rapture | remittance |
| rating | renounce |
| readily | renown |
| realize | repetition |
| realm | replies |
| reasonable | representative |

*Advanced List Continued*

### 751-775

1. To **rescue** Carver was quite a **responsibility** because Gorman, **revolver** in hand, stood on a **ridge** and could easily **riddle** anyone who came near.
2. **Respective** doctors had told His **Reverence** that the pain seemed to **resemble rheumatism,** but he thought the idea **ridiculous.**
3. His **reputation** forced him to **resign** rather than **reverse** himself and **retreat** from a position he considered beyond **reproach.**
4. Since the decision of the **revenue** agent to tax your **reserve** fund is not **reversible,** thoughts of **revenge** will not **resolve** your difficulty.
5. Pancho **reveled** in the **restless** spirit of **resistance** that no one could **restrain** from becoming **revolutionary** in action.

### 776-800

1. We tried to be **sanitary,** but containers were **scarce** and we had to **rinse** out **salmon** or **sardine** cans and use them.
2. If the **rumor** that he had sold his **scheme** to the enemy were true, it would **ruin** the **scientist** and might cause a **riot.**
3. It must give that **rooster satisfaction** to keep his **schedule** because he will **rouse** us at dawn even on the **Sabbath.**
4. To call his **salve** a **sample** of the **sacred** ointment was bad enough, but to make it **salable** was **sacrilegious.**
5. On his **route** to the ranch, Chambers found a **savage** wild horse that took all his **science** to **saddle** in **satisfactory** fashion.

## *Advanced List Continued*

| | |
|---|---|
| reproach | rinse |
| reputation | riot |
| rescue | rooster |
| resemble | rouse |
| reserve | route |
| resign | ruin |
| resistance | rumor |
| resolve | Sabbath |
| respective | sacred |
| responsibility | sacrilegious |
| restless | saddle |
| restrain | salable |
| retreat | salmon |
| reveled | salve |
| revenge | sample |
| revenue | sanitary |
| reverence | sardine |
| reverse | satisfaction |
| reversible | satisfactory |
| revolutionary | savage |
| revolver | scarce |
| rheumatism | schedule |
| riddle | scheme |
| ridge | science |
| ridiculous | scientist |

## Advanced List Continued
### 801-825

1. A **sedative** and short rest on the **sofa** calmed the **seamstress** who had let out a **shriek** when the gas flame began **singeing** her hair.
2. Last **semester**, at the **settlement** house, a **socialist** delivered a **series** of talks on subjects in which he **sincerely** believed.
3. With a **sigh**, Mr. Walton agreed with his friend, **Sergeant** Peters, that the painting **situated** in the **social** hall would have to be freshly **shellacked**.
4. The **shrewd** salesman was so **skillful** he could convince the most **sensible** that the **site** for their home was **similar** to the best.
5. All the **shepherd** did was **snatch** a pair of **shears** and cut the **slippery serpent** in two.

### 826-850

1. With a **solemn** nod, Mr. Ford revived Sally's **spirits** when he **specified** he would use enough **starch** to make her dresses **sparkle**.
2. We watched Mr. Gates **stalk** about the **stable** and **stare** at every corner because the **squirrel** was still **somewhere** around.
3. The **splendor** of a **spectacle** involving twenty **stately** sopranos singing together could **stagger** the imagination.
4. To **solve** the problem, he would tie every **solitary squash** to a **stake** and then **sprinkle** each with the insect powder.
5. Her **stationary** work and daily **solitude** made the **sphere** of interest of the old **spinner somewhat** limited.

*Advanced List Continued*

seamstress

sedative

semester

sensible

sergeant

series

serpent

settlement

shears

shellacked

shepherd

shrewd

shriek

sigh

similar

sincerely

singeing

site

situated

skillful

slippery

snatch

social

socialist

sofa

solemn

solitary

solitude

solve

somewhat

somewhere

sopranos

sparkle

specified

spectacle

sphere

spinner

spirits

splendor

sprinkle

squash

squirrel

stable

stagger

stake

stalk

starch

stare

stately

stationary

*Advanced List Continued*

## 851-875

1. Although **successful** in stealing **stationery** from the **studios**, he was too **stupid** to see he was **subtly** being given rope to hang himself.
2. The **substance** of the speech by the **superintendent** was that he would **strengthen** the **strict** application of the **statute** against smoking.
3. **Sulphur** fumes caused him to **stumble** on his way up the **steeple**, but his **stubborn** will was **sufficient** to keep him from falling.
4. Her **sullen** reaction to the **suggestion** by the **supervisor** to **stitch** the new pattern carefully was **suitable** reason for her dismissal.
5. As we passed the **strait**, the crew had to **subdue** a **stowaway** who had tried to force the cook to **surrender** a jar of **strawberry** jam.

## 876-900

1. When **testimony** revealed that the **switchman** could not have been near the **tavern**, the **surrogate** showed some **sympathy** and resumed reading the will.
2. The orders were to **surround** the **tannery** where the **teamster** worked and to hide in a **thicket** until the **suspect** came out.
3. **Symmetry** in design was no **temporary symbol** to the **textile** firms, but a permanent reminder that this would **sustain** their business.
4. To **tease** the **thirsty** boys, Sis poured some **syrup** into a glass and added milk, **thereby** making them mad with **temptation**.
5. When we **surveyed** the **temperature** on the **thermometer**, we realized that even in the **temperate** zone an occasional **tempest** was possible.

*Advanced List Continued*

| | |
|---|---|
| stationery | surrogate |
| statute | surround |
| steeple | surveyed |
| stitch | suspect |
| stowaway | sustain |
| strait | switchman |
| strawberry | symbol |
| strengthen | symmetry |
| strict | sympathy |
| stubborn | syrup |
| studios | tannery |
| stumble | tavern |
| stupid | teamster |
| subdue | tease |
| substance | temperate |
| subtly | temperature |
| successful | tempest |
| sufficient | temporary |
| suggestion | temptation |
| suitable | testimony |
| sullen | textile |
| sulphur | thereby |
| superintendent | thermometer |
| supervisor | thicket |
| surrender | thirsty |

*Advanced List Continued*

### 901-925

1. In the **tragedy** of Caesar, we read how he returned in **triumph** and was **thrice** offered the **throne** by the Roman **throng**.
2. Whenever the **trumpet** announced a new **tributary** in the parade, it seemed to **torture** the **traitor** Cassius and make him **tremble** with rage.
3. Mr. Brice contracted **tonsillitis** trying to arrange **transportation** for every **trifle** contributed to swell the **treasury** of the **tuberculosis** fund.
4. We could **translate** the **twinkle** in the baron's eye as meaning he would forget the **tradition** of no **trespassing** on this lovely June **twilight**.
5. His **type** loved to **torment** others, and he would even **tread** on a **turtle** and **trample** it for the pleasure it gave him.

### 926-950

1. People would **vanish** into a secret **vault** under a **veil** of secrecy if they excited the **vengeance** of the old **tyrant**.
2. Unfortunately, in trying to keep the **ukulele underneath** the **umbrella**, Don dropped his **valise**.
3. **Ventilate** the room well because children **usually** regard the need to **vaccinate** them as **unnecessary tyranny** and are likely to **faint**.
4. His lack of **vanity** made him **uncertain** about how **usable** his **verse** would be, but it turned out to have **unexpected** merit.
5. When we did **venture** into the room, we found the **upholsterer**, almost **unconscious**, sitting **upright** on a pile of **velvet**.

*Advanced List Continued*

thrice

throne

throng

tonsillitis

torment

torture

tradition

tragedy

traitor

trample

translate

transportation

tread

treasury

tremble

trespassing

tributary

trifle

triumph

trumpet

tuberculosis

turtle

twilight

twinkle

type

tyranny

tyrant

ukulele

umbrella

uncertain

unconscious

underneath

unexpected

unfortunately

unnecessary

upholsterer

upright

usable

usually

vaccinate

valise

vanish

vanity

vault

veil

velvet

vengeance

ventilate

venture

verse

*Advanced List Continued*

### 951-975

1. The **victorious warrior** used a trick **whereby** he was able to **whirl** the **villain** over his head and cast him down to defeat.

2. **Wherefore** such a **vulgar** display of **violence** arose over a slight **violation** was the ground **wherein** our complaint was lodged.

3. Far from the **wholesome** outer world, the **witch** retired into the **wilderness whither** she could **worship** her evil spirits.

4. **Whoever** sees **womenfolk weave** cloth in poor light should warn them of the **weakness** of **vision** that may result.

5. **Whew**, letting that part of the tube **wither** away is **voluntary** on your part, but I would **vulcanize** it with some **virgin** rubber.

### 976-990

1. Nothing could **wrinkle** the **worsted** which was as soft as a spring **zephyr**.

2. So great was his **wrath** that the **wretched** boy would not **yield** though badly beaten.

3. The **Zulu** chief placed a **wreath** like a **yoke** around my neck.

4. As a relief from his **zoological** studies, Terry took a piece of **zwieback** and went over to play the **xylophone**.

5. If you believe in signs of the **zodiac**, those **zinnia** plants of **yours** will do well this year.

*Advanced List Continued*

| | |
|---|---|
| victorious | wilderness |
| villain | witch |
| violation | wither |
| violence | womenfolk |
| virgin | worship |
| vision | worsted |
| voluntary | wrath |
| vulcanize | wreath |
| vulgar | wretched |
| warrior | wrinkle |
| weakness | xylophone |
| weave | yield |
| whereby | yoke |
| wherefore | yours |
| wherein | zephyr |
| whew | zinnia |
| whirl | zodiac |
| whither | zoological |
| whoever | Zulu |
| wholesome | zwieback |

# INDEX

266

# Instruction Guide

*Six Minutes a Day to Perfect Spelling* combines the best of contemporary thinking in the field of spelling instruction with original suggestions and devices prepared by the author. Basically, the guiding pedagogic principle is the "test-study-test" approach, which is designed to diagnose the errors, adopt remedial measures, and examine the results of the learning process.

The book concentrates its attention largely on how the poor speller can most effectively overcome his difficulties by a method of study which makes words "part of him." There is, too, an abundance of diagnostic and testing material, both in the sentences found in the Appendix and the paragraphs used as chapter summaries.

Since the word lists have been graded, the use of the book is not restricted to any one school level. The "Basic Word List" contains samples that are suitable for elementary and junior high school students, the "Average List" for junior and senior high school classes, and the "Advanced List" for as high as the university level where the author used it extensively with adult groups. The words were collated from existing scientific studies, state syllabi, school texts, and college surveys, including the Pollack analysis at New York University.

Every teacher of spelling undoubtedly has pet devices which have proved useful in the past, and we do not presume that the suggestions that follow are the definitive answers to the very real problem our youngsters face as they try to master our rather inconsistent language. However, the proposed methods of using the material have been carefully checked in classroom situations, and should serve certainly as *additional* means of realizing our common objective.

Listed here are ideas that can be used with the book:

√ Almost all authorities agree that it is undesirable to spend full periods on spelling. Rather it should be taught functionally, as the need arises with the individual student, or in short, frequently-spaced lessons. Both the "Daily Plan" and "Long Range Plan" should fit into this system very well. The teacher can utilize the suggested notebook arrangement and word-accumulation plan on a class as well as individual basis.

√ Possibly the chart found in the "Ninety Day Trial" can become a permanent outline on a side blackboard, and be used for daily entry of particular problem words. The youngsters can devote three minutes in the morning, during the home room period, to their first attack on the word; can be encouraged to spend a second few minutes with the SEE-THINK-FEEL system during their study periods; and be assigned further to complete their third study of the word at home. Some students, preferably the better ones who do not need extensive drill, can be asked to volunteer to compose practice sentences and paragraphs containing the words listed in the daily chart described above. This approach offers motivation at all levels, and provides the teacher readily with testing material prepared by the students themselves.

√ As additional extra-credit work, students (in this case preferably the weaker ones) can be aske dto bring in colored charts showing problem words presented as suggested in the chapter on "See the Word."

√ Occasionally, a few minutes can be spent asking the class to come up with a good "bond" for a word (See "Think the Word"). Some recognition may be given the ones who supply the best association patterns.

√ The better students may be assigned the task of helping others, especially in the reading of test paragraphs, the guiding of "Tracing" drills (See "Feel the Word"), and the marking of results.

√ The "spellograms" can be fun for the youngsters, and it is suggestde that the team games outlined in the chapter on spelling games become regular parts of classroom routine. A league within a class may even be formed, daily contests held, and league standings posted prominently where the day to day won and lost records can be followed with interest by the contestants.

√The chapter on word histories can be the springboard for adventures in words. Pupils who prepare little etymological stories can combine with others who have talent in art work. Some highly striking illustrations can be prepared. For example, one person may, let us say, draw a picture of Tantalus surrounded by water and overhanging branches of fruit, another prepare the story behind the name, and a third do the lettering of a typical derived word (TANTALIZE), thus explaining why the problem A after the second T exists.

√With the present interest in audio-visual aids, some thought can be given to the preparation of slides for projection. These can be used with the "See the Word" technique. Recordings, as indicated by Spellick #2, can be made of sample sentences and paragraphs. This can become a joint undertaking of the English and Speech departments. The resultant novelty and uniformity of presentation of test material to the classes will create added interest, besides relieving the teacher of the burden of dictation.

√An interesting schoolwide project can be tried. The English Department can determine what ten words are most troublesome within each grade. A poster contest can then be initiated providing for entries within the grades, followed by competition among them all. Prizes can be awarded to grade winners as well as to the top three in the school. Many of the posters can be attached in rotating order to the bulletin boards in the classrooms, and the grand prize winners' entries can be hung in the school lobby or corridors. A mass program of this kind might well motivate better spelling among students of the entire school.

√The industrial arts or shop departments may be willing to integrate their work with the English Department by permitting poor spellers to construct various "spellicks" as part of their required work for the term. These students can receive a mark from the shop teacher for the quality of their construction, and be further rewarded by the English teacher for making the effort to improve their spelling.

Insofar as the use of the book as a unit is concerned, the author wishes to recommend a procedure which, so far as he knows, is not in use in any of the schools. Teachers know, of course, that for some years considerable attention has been paid to remedial reading. Admittedly the problem in this area is extensive and demands concerted effort on the part of the educators. It is the opinion of the author, however, that there is an equally large number of students who need help in spelling. Schools might well consider the advisability of setting up *remedial spelling classes* in the same manner as reading groups are formed. A full term devoted to the practices outlined in *Six Minutes a Day to Perfect Spelling* should be rewarding for those who may otherwise pass on to adulthood with poor spelling plaguing their writing efforts.

In classes where poor spellers are in the minority, students may be advised to get the book and work with the more expert writers. A daily review of one word can be worked into the schedule. The pupil "teacher" can dictate a trial sentence while the attendance is being taken, in this way testing the results of the poor speller's study the previous day.

May we invite those teachers who find some use for *Six Minutes a Day to Perfect Spelling* to pass on to us the results of their experiences with it, along with any suggestions for improvement that may occur to them. It is our aim to provide a learning tool for the schools, and we are fully aware of the contribution teachers can make in advising us of its effectiveness.